Golden Giving - Everything You Need to Know for an Enriched, Socially Conscious Retirement

Golden Giving - Everything You Need to Know for an Enriched, Socially Conscious Retirement

Vasudevan Rajaram, Keith Olson and Andrea Groner

© 2017 Vasudevan Rajaram, Keith Olson and Andrea Groner
All rights reserved.

ISBN: 1975951417
ISBN 13: 9781975951412

Contents

Preface vii

Introduction xi

Chapter 1 Taking Care of Yourself to Take Care of Others 1

Chapter 2 Finding Your Cause: Defining Your Values for Successful Philanthropy 35

Chapter 3 Giving Locally 55

Chapter 4 Opportunities and Challenges Internationally 76

Chapter 5 Nonprofit Organizations 102

Chapter 6 New Mediums of Giving 132

Chapter 7 Fundraising 144

Chapter 8	Inspirational Stories	165
Chapter 9	Suggested Action Plan	178
	Bibliography	185
	Acknowledgements	193
	Appendix A: How to Analyze a Nonprofit Entity	195
	Appendix B—Formation of a 501(c)(3) Organization	197
	About the Author	199

Preface

Humans need purpose in their lives to feel emotionally satisfied. When we are working, we feel satisfied by our professional accomplishments, and we are busy raising our children or just enjoying life. When we retire, our sense of purpose may become harder to see, and we must try to fill our lives with meaningful things. This book is a guide to finding purpose in your retirement and giving back to society in your local community or in any part of the world. However, you must have the resources to give back, so chapter 1 of this book describes how you can plan for a healthy and wealthy retirement by taking care of yourself physically and financially. A section is also devoted to how you can spend time in spiritual pursuits during your retirement.

We will present many ideas for giving back in your local community and within the United States. There is a lot of unmet need in our inner cities and rural areas, and opportunities to serve this need are discussed in this book as well. The opportunities for volunteering your time, talents, and treasure are many, and you have to choose what fits your interest and passion to serve. For example, I (Rajaram) joined the Lions Club in my community a decade ago, and it has been fun serving the needy in my community and enjoying the company of others who are keen to serve others. I look forward to every Lions Club meeting and the service projects we take on.

Chapter 2 of this book is devoted to finding your cause. Many of the world's religions emphasize charity and helping your fellow human beings in need. After reflection upon your values and the needs in your community, you can decide to help in a food pantry, an organization serving youth, a group helping the homeless, or a service club like the Lions or Rotary. Any of these opportunities to serve will enrich your life as much as or more than the help you provide to the organization. I can tell you this from personal experience, and the wonderful people I have met and who have enriched my life are many.

Chapter 3 provides myriads of opportunities to give back to causes within the United States. The causes described range from hunger to homelessness, from environment to music, and many areas where one may provide their skills, time and money. Special mention is made of service organizations that serve many unmet needs in communities ranging far and wide, from rural communities to inner city neighborhoods.

In chapter 4, we will discuss opportunities available and challenges you will face when you serve an international organization that is based in the United States and serves the poor in other countries. Diaspora giving is promoted by the US Agency for International Development, and many opportunities for engagement are available through the International Diaspora Engagement Alliance (www.diasporaalliance.org). Workshops and many other forms of free assistance are provided to anyone interested in giving in Africa, the Caribbean, and Latin America. US citizens come from many parts of the world, and the easiest way to do this is to engage in the country of your origin. I have been involved in giving back to India for more than ten years and can attest to the pleasure to be had from seeing donor dollars go a long way toward helping many causes, such as education, skills development, and health care.

Chapter 5 provides information about how to join or assist an existing nonprofit organization. Since there are over 1.5 million tax-exempt organizations in the United States, understanding how they operate and how effective they are in serving the needy is important before you decide which one to work with. Once you choose an organization to devote your energy to, you must determine what opportunities are available to work with them so that you use your talents, time, and treasure effectively. Information is provided on types of nonprofit organizations, how to evaluate them, and how to work with them so that you can do what you have always wanted to do but did not have time to do.

Chapter 6 is devoted to the new types of philanthropy available to people who want to serve the needs of society, including crowd funding, microfinance, philanthrocapitalism, and social entrepreneurship. You may wish to use these new mediums of giving to serve the unmet needs of society that you want to address. Even if you want to help an individual or a family or a community need, these new mediums of giving can help you accomplish your goal.

Fund-raising is a critical component of any effort you undertake to help society. Chapter 7 tells you how to raise funds from various types of donors. If you just want to donate to a cause and meet a fund raiser who wants you to donate to a cause, guidance is provided to ask the right questions so that your dollars will be put to the best use by the organization. Most people I meet say that it is hard to ask for funds from others for a cause you believe in, but after you read this chapter, you will understand that you are giving the donor an opportunity to serve people whom he or she wanted to help but did not know how to do effectively.

A lot of inspirational stories are provided in chapter 8. These will get you started on your journey of purpose to help the needy. We share stories of people who have given back in India, Uganda, and in their community in the United States. These stories show that you can start at any age and launch your journey of service. Networking with other nonprofits already doing great work in the part of the world you are interested in and in the cause in which you want to be involved is one way of leveraging your time, talent, and treasure for the maximum impact.

Chapter 9 provides an action plan that will help you get involved in a life of service and giving to others who are in need. We will discuss the benefits to your psyche and well-being along with practical steps for you to live a life of purpose and serve others. Some of the key points in the book are again emphasized in this chapter.

A bibliography and sources of information are provided for you to do further research and find the path best suited to you when you want to get involved and give back to society. Appendix A gives details of how to analyze a non-profit organizations before donating money to them. Appendix B tells you how to start your own non-profit organization. The authors hope that this will help you get the most of your retirement years and impact many lives around the world.

Introduction

All of us want to lead purposeful lives, but during the busiest periods of our lives, we tend to forget our purpose and feel frustrated with our daily battles. We feel stressed, and we try to manage our responsibilities the best way we can during those years. However, once our kids are grown up and independent, we can start refocusing our purpose in this world and do things that fulfill our life's purpose. This book will give you many options—available in the United States and around the world—to give back and feel purposeful. It will also give you many ways that you can take care of yourself so that you are in a position to give back to society. You will read many inspirational stories of people who are giving back in their retirement years and changing lives.

According to Hindu culture, our lives have four major phases: Learning, Earning, Giving, and Getting Ready for Salvation. Each of these four phases is described below.

Learning

From our birth, we are learning things, and this usually continues until age twenty-five. We acquire the skills to make a living and become independent of our parents. Although learning continues throughout our life, we get our basic degrees and skills for joining the work force in the first twenty-five years of our life. Although we learn a little about giving back through community volunteering programs and service learning programs in college, these are brief and sporadic.

Earning

From about age twenty-five to sixty, we are focused on starting our own business, busy in the workforce, or climbing the corporate ladder. We get married, start families, and help our children grow to be good citizens. Some of us take care of our older parents. Some help relatives and friends who need help. All these activities consume much of our time and financial resources, and we often don't have time to think of those less fortunate in our community or have the financial resources to donate to causes that are close to our heart.

Giving Back

From the ages of sixty to eighty, many of us have the time and resources to help others in our community and to support favorite causes—local, national, and international. The authors have used this time to support local, national, and international causes while enjoying their retirement doing other things like travel and time with grandchildren. This book is focused on relating our personal experiences and also providing stories of others who have given back in many ways to society.

Getting Ready for Salvation

From eighty to the time we leave the planet, we are supposed to be more spiritually oriented and devote time to prayer and spiritual activities (which could include social service). As our health starts to fail, the focus on spirituality allows us to adjust to what may come and be ready for death.

Other religions have their own phases of life, but all of them have their *golden rules*:

1. Do unto others what you would have others do to you.
2. Be compassionate, kind, and giving (Christians and Mormons suggest 10 percent of income as a giving goal).
3. The five pillars of faith in Islam include charitable giving as a necessary component of being a good Muslim.

There are many books that describe the ways one can help solve problems in the United States and around the world. They often present a lot of statistics about philanthropy and how you can participate in giving back to society. The main objective of our book is to show by example that it is possible to take care of yourself *and* be ready to make the best out of your retirement years.

The talents possessed by people in their sixties are varied, and if we can mobilize these talents and the financial resources they have, many problems in the local, national, and international arena can be solved. We can live in a better world full of hope. This book is our attempt to mobilize the time, talent, and treasure of people in their sixties to improve our world. We hope it helps you lead a purposeful life and encourages you to get involved in helping others who are less fortunate than you.

When You Are Ready to Give Back

Once you are close to retirement, you will likely be wondering what you will do in your retirement years, which could last as long as twenty years or more. After you have read chapter 1 and feel you are ready to give back, ask yourself these questions:

1. How much time will I have after I budget time for my family, including my grandchildren?

2. What is my passion, and how do I want to use it to help others, both in the United States and abroad?
3. What are my talents, and how can I use them to help people in my community and around the world?
4. How much money do I have to give to charities, and do I want to participate in legacy giving to my favorite charity?
5. Given the state of my health, where do I want to focus my energies in giving back?

Everyone is unique, and the options for giving back are numerous. Some people move close to their children and spend all their time taking care of the grandchildren. Some people have elderly parents who live with them or in a nearby nursing home and are busy taking care of them and their grandchildren, leaving them no time to give back. Such people are taking care of their responsibilities fully and giving their time and resources to help with the next generation. However, if you don't have these responsibilities, your range of opportunities to give back is vast. The answers to the above questions will determine how you give back.

Charitable giving in the United States is mostly by individuals, and about 20 percent is from corporate foundations. We are the most charitable country in the world—giving exceeded $350 billion in 2015.

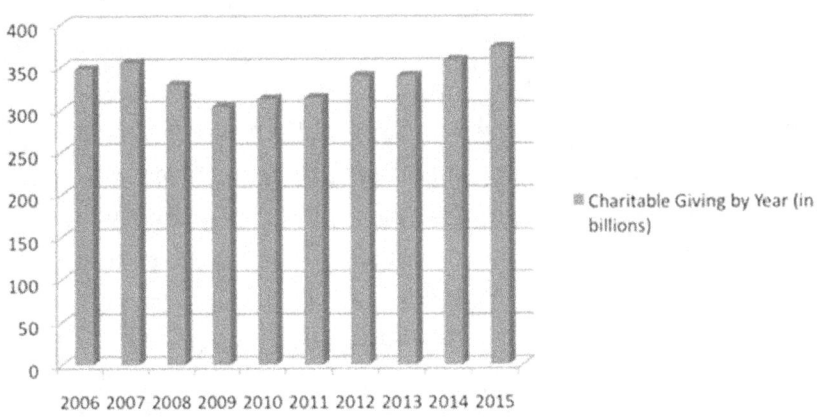

As you can see in the graph above, by the year 2015, charitable giving had recovered from the 2008 financial crash and returned to its prerecession levels. (Data taken from *Giving USA Report 2015.*)

Let us look at the above questions in depth. Regarding the first question, unless your children need you to help with your grandchildren on a daily basis, it is better to spend some quality time with them and devote the rest to the needs of your local community. Parents like to spend time with their children and bring them up in their own way. Respect that, and provide your time as and when needed. There are many causes that can benefit from your time, talent, and treasure, and once you prioritize the causes, you will have your plan of action. The needs in most communities are many; you must decide which one is closest to your heart and most convenient to you. For me, it was hunger and education. Hence, I selected the Greater Chicago Food Depository in Chicago, tutoring/mentoring in Chicago, and supporting an education nonprofit in India, the country of my birth. I decided to spend a minimum of 40 percent of my time and 10 percent of my income to support these causes. I also learned fund-raising and started collecting funds from the community to support an education nonprofit in India.

Another excuse we often hear from retirees is that they have to travel to places and do the things on their bucket list. There are only so many hours you can do this, and you can still find time to get involved in giving back. I found that even with a busy life during my working years, with a young daughter and a busy wife, I could find two hours a week to tutor a young student who needed guidance to finish high school. In two years, spending less than one hundred hours a year, I helped this young girl finish school and be admitted to the University of Illinois–Chicago. Most of all, it made me very happy to see that my voluntary work helped a young girl launch her life and be the first one in her family to finish school and go to college. So you can find time for community service even while satisfying your bucket list of things you want to do.

Finding your passion requires a lot of reflection, so that you can find the one or two things that make you excited to get up every day and do your best. Getting involved in these causes has several benefits to yourself as well as to the persons you serve. You find meaning in your retirement years and stay healthy, since you will have a regular routine similar to the one you had during your working years. Especially since many of us are living into our eighties and nineties, this is very necessary to lead a healthy and happy life. This book describes the many ways you can get involved in your community, in the United States, and around the world. We regularly hear about people who are doing amazing things with their retirement years and helping many in need. The inspirational stories chapter describes Dr. Prakasam Tata and many others. Dr. Tata is eighty-one years old but feels a lot younger since he works on Rotary Club projects in his community and in India, where he goes for three months every year. He indulges in his passion for clean water and sanitation and keeps technically abreast of improvements in his field.

Passion for helping others is the main requirement for you to get involved, and this can be enhanced by joining groups that are already serving the community. In addition, reading good books and websites like www.servicespace.org and www.dailygood.org can inspire you to find the passion within you. There are so many inspiring stories of ordinary people rising to extraordinary levels of giving by using their passion to help others.

We all have multiple talents, and you have to list them to see which of these talents is required in your community and in other parts of the country and abroad. If you like working with children, you can find a need in the community to tutor/mentor children. If you are good with numbers, you can help a nonprofit organization in your community with budgeting and tax preparation. Once you start volunteering for various causes, you will discover talents that you didn't know you had. For example, I had no idea I had fund-raising skills, but when I started doing it, I enjoyed it and now encourage others to raise funds for their causes. I enjoy the challenge and am constantly learning of ways to raise money. I have been able to raise close to a million dollars in the past few years.

All development projects need money, and you have to be careful which group you give your donations to. Some groups spend less than 10 percent of the money they receive on administration and fund-raising, devoting the rest to helping the people for whom they are raising money. Other groups spend over 50 percent on salaries, office space, and fund-raising, and their impact is considerably less than the organizations that are frugal and focused on the cause. You can review the 990 Form submitted by the charity to the Internal Revenue Service (IRS). The way to review a 990 Form is provided in Appendix A. A thorough review will tell you a lot about the charity's finances, its management and operations, and other information as to how effective the charity is in serving the poor.

Charity Navigator is a great website that lists more than seven thousand US charities that raise over a million dollars year after year for two years or more, Using the site's rating system is useful in deciding whom to give your hard earned dollars to. It rates charities by a star-rating system, with the top four-star rating given to charities that spend 10 percent or less of the funds collected for administration and fund-raising. You can give to charities that have a four-star rating and ones that you know personally through friends or have seen their work personally. You can give 10 percent of your resources to charities you care for. In addition to money, you can give your time and talent, which will make a bigger impact on causes dear to you. A chapter in this book is devoted to raising funds for your charity.

As the old saying goes, *Health is wealth.* If you have good health, you can help others while helping yourself gain peace of mind and satisfaction that you can improve others' lives. If you are in good health, you can travel to places around the world where they need your talents and time. Many organizations, such as Rotary Club and Lions Club, are always looking for volunteers to help in the various causes they are involved in around the world. If your health and finances will only permit you to travel locally in your community, you can do that and gain a lot of happiness. True joy lies in selfless service, so whatever your health status, you can help others and reap happiness. Chapter 1 of this book is devoted to taking care of your physical, mental, spiritual and financial health.

CHAPTER 1

Taking Care of Yourself to Take Care of Others

Part I: Taking Care of Yourself—General Health

If you're reading this book, you're interested in volunteering. And what should be your first project/cause? Did you put yourself first? That's right! You're not being selfish—if you don't have your affairs in order, it's hard to do the right things for others. And what should you take care of first—health, relations with others, or finances? Did you answer *all of those*? Right again! That's what this chapter is all about. Feel free to skip to other chapters if you're confident you're fine, but keep reading if you are not so sure.

> Key fact I: Nobody lives forever.
> Key fact II: You don't know how long you will live.

Consider this. Maybe you're fine one day, and the next you break a hip and you're on a downhill slide. Maybe you're feeling fine one day, and the next you find you have stage IV cancer and need hospice. Maybe you realize you shouldn't be driving and wonder how you'll adjust to this new reality.

Kind of gloomy? If you're in your mid-sixties, you know life can be less than cheerful. Probably you have friends who have been seriously ill. If you've got things in good order, you'll be able to adjust better. Test yourself with the following checklist:

Do you

1. have regular medical checkups?
2. exercise?
3. eat sensibly?
4. smoke?
5. drink moderately (if you drink at all)?
6. keep expenses in check and know your financial status?
7. stay active and involved, mentally and physically?
8. maintain good relations with family and friends?
9. have plans for the future?

Let's take these items one at a time, but briefly, as you likely know and have heard lots of good advice (and probably some bad advice) about all of these. There's plenty of information available in books and magazines and on the Internet, not all of it trustworthy. One book I recommend is *Winning Strategies for Successful Aging*, by Eric Pfeiffer (Yale University Press, 2013). The book is long enough to cover most of the checklist but short enough that you don't get bogged down. Dr. Pfeiffer also throws in personal tales to bring home the general advice.

1. Regular medical checkups
These should keep you in better health and may save you money, even your life, by catching a problem when it's still small and treatable. You'll have less anguish if you know about your health, for better or worse. Have your hearing checked, if only as a benchmark.

A checkup on your living space can reduce the chances of a fall. Are there trip hazards? Maybe you're living with clutter or even hoarding. The stuff you've accumulated can get in the way of doing things. Organize it and reduce it while you're in good shape to do so.

And don't forget regular trips to the dentist. Regular brushing and flossing and checkups can save your teeth and gums. Do you know anyone with dentures? You know what a chore those are—you can't chew as well, and when they're not in you don't speak clearly. Even the best ones, well maintained, are no substitute for real choppers. If you have a tooth that's too far gone to save, consider an implant. Expensive? Sure, very expensive, but it is money well spent. None of the alternatives are as solid, whether a bridge or dentures.

2. Exercise

Regular exercise is the key. You don't need to run marathons—walking and bicycling are good, as is swimming, and yoga can help keep joints loose. And it doesn't have to be expensive either. Some health plans offer Silver Sneakers, a free fitness program for seniors. For most of us, just doing it is a roadblock. Marking what you've done, perhaps on a handy calendar, can help keep you honest. Consider joining a group, perhaps a yoga class, or link up with folks who exercise regularly. Or do some errands on foot. You think that will take too long? Here's a counter-argument—if an errand takes fifteen minutes by car and thirty on foot, do the math. Walk and you've gotten thirty minutes of exercise in only fifteen minutes longer than using the car.

An acquaintance of mine, a retired MD, says his physician recommends walking half an hour a day. That's good advice—something to stick to. *Ah, there's the rub.* How do you stick to it? Maybe make it social; take a daily walk with friends. Maybe join the local Y or a health club, where you'll make friends. Maybe keep a chart where you can see that you're on track. How about walking to your local coffee shop or to do errands? And walking is not the only a good way to exercise, swimming is great, and so is bicycling. What about using those machines at the health club and throwing in a little resistance (weight) effort? Could be regular weights, but it doesn't have to be fancy. You can even exercise at home by squeezing a tennis ball, lifting a book a bunch of times, or using a milk jug. A half full gallon jug, handle included, is four pounds, and the weight is easy to adjust to your ability—just add or subtract water. Don't overdo it; just do it.

3. Don't smoke and maintain a smoke free living space

The evidence is clear: smoking is horrible for you. If you've ever seen a picture of the lung of a long-time smoker, you wouldn't even be a short-time smoker. Still a smoker? When you were twenty-five, you knew you were immortal and cigarettes couldn't hurt you. Now you know better. If you still smoke, you don't need to be told it's not good for you, and you probably know relatives and friends who are handicapped by smoking. Do you want to be short of breath all the time or have to tote a portable oxygen tank everywhere you go? Of course not. But habits are tough to break.

How to get started? Get the patch. Substitute something, perhaps gum. Avoid situations where smoking is part of the routine. If that means a smoke break at work, and you've stopped working, you're already halfway there. Part of the appeal of smoking is social. If you join a group of others who gave it up, you'll have the social without the smoking—you'll reinforce each other's good habits.

4. Moderate alcohol consumption

You like your drink? By itself, this is not a problem; in fact; moderation is good. People who have a drink or two a day live longer on average than those who don't drink and those who drink more than a couple. As with smoking, if you're drinking more than you should, cut back on bar visits or substitute something. Tea, anyone? Socialize in other ways than the bar scene. If you have a real problem, get help.

5. Finances
This is a tough one. Most of us didn't start saving enough early enough. Many of us don't want to talk about it. Maybe we aren't good with numbers, or deep down we think it's out of our control. What's a good place to start to make sure your finances are in order? A rough idea of how much you have, your valuation or net worth, your income and expenses, is important. Imagine yourself as a business. A business will have a balance sheet (for you, your valuation) and a profit and loss statement (for you, income and expenses). Your figuring doesn't have to be complicated or take much time. A rough idea is good enough.

6. Stay active and involved, mentally and spiritually
Play cards or board games, go to concerts or plays, or maybe join a theater group. Take a class; be active in an organization. You don't need to be fussy about the activity—getting out and about is good, and there are even some activities to pursue that involve staying at home. There's something for everyone.

7. Maintain good relations with family and friends.
Family and friends are your most important asset, and reaching out to them enriches your life. If you do have a crisis, medical or otherwise, they can be there to help you, but you need to be on good terms now.

8. Have plans for the future.
All the advice folk say get a will or even a trust. My father had a small estate, mainly the value of his house, but a trust made closing that estate much easier than would have been the case without a will.

Do you procrastinate about any of these things? If you did before, now's not the time.

Part II: Food and Diet

While you were working, you may not have had the time to watch your food choices. Time to rearrange those? Eating well needn't be a struggle, you don't have to be a gourmet chef, in fact you likely can eat better for less money with only minimal effort. Example, a simple rice dish takes only half an hour, start to finish, and much of that time is letting the rice cook while you do other things.

Eating the right stuff is simple; eating properly is complicated. Sound contradictory? It is, but let's make sense of the contradiction. Starting with the simple, you need energy, you need some vital nutrients. Both of those come from only five categories of food, carbohydrates, proteins, fats, vitamins and minerals, and you need some of each. Carbohydrates provide energy. Something from each of the other four is essential though the good news is that a decent diet gives you what you need. That any food you eat is a mixture of some of those five means it's easy to get what you should have. Eat an orange and you get energy and vitamin C as well as fiber.

What's good to do? You've heard and know most of it - eat more vegetables and fruits. Grains are good, especially whole grains. What's not good? Excess dairy and meat consumption, particularly red meat. You can reduce sugar and fat, the description 'empty calories' applies to both, as well as salt. Author Michael Pollan has a seven word directive, "Eat food. Not too much. Mostly plants." Two added words, 'take walks', adds more good sense.

What can you do for good healthy eating, an alternative to the Standard American Diet (SAD) ? There's lots of dietary advice available, not all of it reliable, but a good start would be the DASH diet which focuses on blood pressure, the letters stand for Dietary Approach to Stop Hypertension, but it's also heart healthy and may help with weight loss. The Mediterranean Diet which also features flavors to love makes a lot of sense and you'll find good guidelines in Michael Pollan's slim book, Food Rules. You don't need to follow all his rules, but they'll get you thinking. The Mayo clinic plugs the DASH diet at mayoclinic.org or try dashdiet.org or library books.

Of course cooking means you'll have to go shopping. The alternatives, restaurants or carry out, don't help with SOS (salt, oil, sugar). In the supermarket reading the labels will help you limit SOS. Tedious? At first it is, but you get the drift quickly and in a short time don't need much time to spot what's good and not. Michael Pollan has a timesaving guideline, shop the outside of a market as that's where you'll find the produce and fresh things. There you'll find the flavonoids, phytochemicals and carotenoids chock full of nutrients. Don't know what those are? Not to worry, my spell check doesn't either, but you get them in colorful foods. By contrast, in the center aisles are the chips and drinks overloaded with salt and sugar, Frozen veggies and fruit are colorful and help redeem those aisles as they combine healthy eating with convenience. Then there are the 'convenience' foods. Often they're not that convenient but the main objection is the stuff in them. SOS again? Probably, but easy to overlook if you don't check labels.

Not all sugar calories are created equal. Some forms go straight to the blood stream, high fructose corn syrup is a common example. The advice from decades ago, 'an apple a day keeps the doctor away' is just as appropriate now as then. You still get the fructose but the apple comes with pulp and fiber that slows the absorption of the sugar,

How you cook things makes a difference. Some old favorites should be reduced or avoided, grilling among them. Fried foods load on the salt and fats, adding calories. Broiling is simple for lots of things - try it for vegetables and fish. Microwaving? Naturally, it is a time saver. Try it with corn - a fresh ear cooks in about minute and a half. Following the directions on a box of rice is simplicity itself.

Will healthy eating cost you? Maybe not, as veggies and beans are less expensive than meat and processed food. Compare the cost of a pound of rice to a pound of steak. Also, what's more expensive, a hospital stay or a healthy diet that keeps you out of the hospital?

If weight loss is your goal, there's a bunch of paragraphs at the end of the chapter that tell you lots. On line, reputable web sites such as mayoclinic.org and cdc.org have helpful hints. And be wary of diets, miracle or not, and the books with the sure-fire method to get healthy and lose weight. If they just get you to lose water, the loss isn't permanent. Calories do count, though you may not have to count calories - just watch what and how much you eat. No two people are identical and the method good for one person might put another in a nutritional straight jacket. You probably know people with diabetes, then there's lactose and gluten intolerance and a host of allergies including the very serious reactions to peanuts and shell fish. Even starch digestion varies considerably depending on ethnic background. Take a look at yours and of course stay alert to your family health history - maybe there's a food intolerance/disease problem there? Real weight loss is inevitably gradual, maybe a pound a week.

For healthy eating, if you reduce sweets and salt and avoid 'bad' fats, you're on your way. Eating more fruits and veggies takes you further. For most of us, easier said than done when you can get a donut at a corner stop, a hamburger from a drive through not far away and the local coffee shop tempts you with sweet treats adding calories to those in a morning latte.

Back to the five categories of food (carbohydrates, proteins, fats, vitamins and minerals)... Except for carbohydrates, which are only for energy, something in the other four is essential though the good news is that a decent diet will give you what you need without worry. Let's take them one at a time.

Carbohydrates:
First let's talk about carbohydrates, or abbreviated, carbs. They have a number of different molecules with roughly two hydrogen and one oxygen atom (you'll remember that's the proportion in water) per one carbon, so the word literally means hydrated carbon. Even if the chemistry isn't quite right, the name stuck, and carbs they are. What we usually call sugar, the white stuff on the table, is sucrose and it's a carb as is fructose; fruit contains fructose as does the common ingredient, high-fructose corn syrup, and there are more, but they're relatively simple molecules and not a good part of healthy eating. The complex carbs we should eat, starch is another name, are just long chains of sugar molecules and take longer to digest. Think of them like a freight train. If you ever waited at a rail crossing for a long train of near identical cars, you've got a good analogy: each car is a simple sugar, the train is a starch. It would take a while to separate all those cars, just as digestive enzymes take time to break apart the starch. By contrast, the simple sugars hit the blood stream with a wallop, calling up a surge of insulin. From peas and beans and rice grains you get the starch, but if it's not heavily processed, you also get significant proteins and valuable fiber. Wood is also a complex carb, cellulose, which we can't digest, hence the low calorie substitute for candy - chew on a toothpick.

There's plenty of nutritional advice warning about the simple carbs. Unfortunately they're everywhere and in multiple forms. Table sugar (sucrose) and high-fructose corn syrup (HFCS) are two and honey and molasses are mostly simple sugars. While there aren't any essential carbohydrates, you need them for energy.

Sugar means calories, but empty calories - no nutrients. Sure, some sugary drinks claim vitamin C, but isn't an orange (or any piece of fruit) better? Another advantage to the fruit is that the fruit sugar (fructose) comes with pulp, spreading out the absorption. We'll talk more about soft drinks when we get to the dieting section.

Proteins:
Much of the body is protein; muscle and blood, skin and brain, just not bones.

The train analogy also works for proteins, just that the cars are more varied as the cars are amino acids. The first amino acid isolated came from asparagus, hence the name asparagine. You may not even know you are familiar with others - the artificial sweetener aspartame, L-Dopa as a treatment for Parkinson's disease and glutamate in MSG. About twenty are present in proteins; some the body can produce but nine are essential and must come from your food. The necessary nine proteins come from animal products, peas and beans, and a mix of grains, wheat, rice and corn and others. And you don't need as much protein as most Americans put on their plate. About 70 grams is sufficient for someone who weighs 180 pounds and you'd get that from eight ounces of any meat. As meats also weigh in with water and fat content, it's difficult to get it exactly right, nor do you need to. You do get a bonus of a couple of nutrients, vitamins and minerals, and excess grams of protein supply energy. You also get fat, more with some meat than other. How much is difficult to pin down, as labeling isn't precise. And you've seen the hamburger that tells you it's 90% lean (which is heavy on protein). What's the other 10%? Fat! Which would you be more likely to buy, ground meat that is 90% lean or a package labeled 10% fat? Of course they're the same.

Fats:
You've heard about saturated and unsaturated fats and know that unsaturated is healthier. To tell which is which is simple - if it's solid at room temperature, it will have more saturated fat. That means oils have more of the healthier unsaturated fats, though note that oils and fats are much the same, it's the ratio of saturated/unsaturated that makes the difference. Labels spell out the amount of each but watch for labeling tricks. One margarine container I saw says 50% less calories than butter. How can that be if calories from one ounce of fat or oil doesn't vary much? The ingredients give the answer - the first is water. Of course that works, whip water into the fat and presto, you've thinned the fat and of course calories go down.

Maybe it's counter intuitive that you need some fat. Omega-3 and omega-6 fats are essential and eating the right things will give you plenty. Most oils have them and the right ratio is also important. Canola oil has an excellent ratio and olive oil is fine; it also is good for heart healthy omega-9. Walnuts, avocados and flax seed all deliver and you can take fish oil pills, but why not just eat some fish? Fried food will give you the wrong ratio and too much fat of the wrong kinds, but eat the right things and you don't need to obsess about what kind of fat you're getting.

Then there are the ones to stay away from, the trans fats. You don't need to know trans fats from transformers to know they're on the no-no list. There are not many around as the government as well as food companies realize they're bad for you and neither wants a bad rap.

And fats are a significant energy source - an ounce of fat delivers twice as many calories as an ounce of either carbs or protein. Good to remember when you wonder what bacon will do to the waistline.

Vitamins and minerals:

Do we need to say much about vitamins? Probably not as good food gives you good vitamins and minerals. Any fruit is loaded with vitamin-C and leafy greens add good minerals, iron included. Do you need a vitamin pill? Not if you eat right but it probably can't hurt, though too many pills combined with various supplements and you can overload. An example is vitamin A, which is essential but too much is toxic. A mineral example most of us aren't aware of is selenium. It's also toxic, very toxic, but also essential. It's an element, right there on the periodic chart you saw in school, and you'll find it in the content list of vitamin pills. Not to worry, you'll get what you need and not be poisoned, with or without the vitamin pill, but a great example that nutrition is both fiendishly complicated but needn't be a bother. However, one mineral that should be a bother is sodium. And salt means sodium and it's ubiquitous. If a list of ingredients says salt, it's sodium - doesn't make any difference what kind, sea salt, iodized salt, it's all sodium. And the 'S' in MSG? That's sodium - MSG is monosodium glutamate. As sodium contributes to high blood pressure, less is better than what most people get. While we can't easily measure how much we're getting, we can do the things that cut our salt intake. Start with banning added salt from the shaker and in cooking, continue with reading labels (you'll be surprised by how 100 grams are in one slice of bread and appalled by how much is in canned soup), and cutting way back. Eating out, from fast food to fine dining, is often high salt eating. Most all processed products, from chips to packaged convenience and microwave food, bring with them loads of salt. Replace with fresh and frozen fruit and veggies and if you want more taste, use what's on a spice rack other than MSG and salt.

If the seasonings, parsley, sage, rosemary and thyme don't appeal to you, would curry, dill, Tabasco and lime be more to your liking?

Keith Olson's Heart Attack

While we were preparing this book, I had a heart attack. While we're all at risk, what were my risk factors? Did I have a family history? Not so much. My father, a lifelong smoker, lived to ninety-two, and my mother lived to eighty-six, though she wouldn't avoid the salt shaker and did have a heart attack. Did I have a bad lifestyle? I never smoked, exercised moderately, mostly walking, and ate sensibly. Even though sensibly meant no added salt, mostly lean meat, and not a lot of sweets or alcohol, I did indulge in cheese and sausage and bread (the salt in bread adds up fast). My BMI (body mass index) was just barely into the overweight range; my cholesterol was also just barely out of recommended range, not enough to take action. Blood pressure was a different matter, as it jerked from no problem to higher than desirable. Still, when I donated blood the Sunday before my midweek attack, it read 120/72, excellent by any standards. Does any of that apply to you? For me, a reasonably healthy lifestyle didn't prevent a medical emergency, but for you it might.

And for me, a heart attack it was. After a rush to the ER and two stents in my clogged coronary arteries, I spent less than twenty-four hours at the hospital, returning home with no major physical restrictions. Regardless, a heart attack is a major jolt—life's not the same. Now, besides the stents and three prescriptions to reduce the things that caused the attack, I have to pay a lot more attention to doing the right thing, especially in terms of diet and exercise. My medical insurance pays for a comprehensive rehab plan, thirty-six sessions of monitored exercise plus short education segments about the heart and lifestyle. The insurance folks figure it's a plus for them if they can keep a person healthy and reduce the chance of another expensive attack. I couldn't agree more. So what's the status? While it's a work in progress, I've kept up the exercise and gone on a strict cardio diet with good results—my total cholesterol is under 100, LDL (the undesirable one, think L for lousy) is way down, and I've lost some weight, though the blood pressure continues to bounce around. Time will tell. And lest you think this is rare and just "my problem," let me tell you that I'm amazed at how many friends have parallel experiences, from stents to bypasses. Might you avoid the tangle of multiple medicines and operations by maintaining a healthy lifestyle? With exercise thrown in, the decades old phrase *an apple a day keeps the doctor away* still applies.

Dieting

Need to lose weight? A majority of people would benefit from shedding pounds, and if that's you, read on. The Centers for Disease Control (CDC) says only a third of people are a suitable weight; another third are overweight, and the final third are obese. Even if those figures are high, lots of people are carrying extra pounds, which means weight that is hard on the knees and increases the risk of disease.

If you want to lose weight, how do you do it and keep it off? Calories are a lot like income and expenses. If you earn more than you spend, you're building cash, which is good. If you're eating more calories than you burn, you're building body weight as fat, which is not good. Dieting is no easy matter, despite the claims of some of the books and TV folks who tout an easy fix. Diet books on the shelves of my local library take up 324 inches. In yards, that's nine, but not the whole nine yards, as there are also yards of cookbooks, some promising a slimmer you. The bookstores have shelves full of fad diets, most of them making unrealistic claims, and you have probably seen the ads claiming you can lose substantial amounts in a short time, maybe ten pounds in ten days. Often those just push pills that cause you to lose water. Pills and fad diets typically don't work for long, and your weight comes back in yo-yo fashion, though I've yet to see a book titled *The Yo-Yo Diet*. Is your problem lack of willpower? Not really—it's the diets that are deficient. What's better? We mentioned the DASH diet earlier, and switching most of your meals to reliance on fruits, vegetables, and whole grains will certainly give you a great start.

Real weight loss means shedding body fat, and the numbers make it difficult, as calories do count. Here's a fat fact worth noting: as energy, a pound of body fat is 3,500 calories. Daily intake for a person is about 2,000 to 2,500 calories, depending on gender, weight, and activity. If you feel you need to lose weight, what can help? The key is reducing calorie intake—calories do count. If you reduce your calorie intake by 500 per day, it will take a week to drop a pound.

For starters, pay attention to your bathroom scale and exercise regularly. By itself, exercise won't do it, but regular exercise will help move some pounds from fat to muscle. As reported in an article in *Scientific American* in February 2017, exercise won't solve a weight problem. Sound contradictory? But exercise is desirable. Another *Scientific American* article, from August 2013, stresses that exercise is good in all sorts of other ways, even improving brain function and reducing the chance of some cancers. And you should consult the scale regularly, though it doesn't have to be every day, even weekly at the same time of day will do. Drop a pound a week, keep it up, and you'll be on your way. Here's a personal story. Decades ago, I had a summer job that required daily walking, not strenuous but lengthy, every day without exception. By the end of the summer, I'd gained five pounds, but my pants were loose. Was I in better shape with or without the five pounds? Obviously some fat got converted to muscle mass, even if my BMI (body mass index) didn't show it.

A note about alcohol. Whether sugars are from grape or grain, when they ferment, alcohol happens, and calories result. Regardless of whether it's beer, wine, or spirits, it's the same kind of alcohol and the same calories. While a glass of wine (or possibly beer) may actually be healthier than teetotalism, the term *beer belly* exists for a reason.

So what's our summary of weight loss and control? Watch what you eat and how much you eat is easy to say; putting those thoughts into practice isn't as easy, though concentrating on healthy foods is a huge help. Regardless, you can't avoid the basics: eat more calories than you use, and you will gain weight. Drop the calories, and you'll drop the pounds.

The books out there about health, especially about diet, typically contain testimonials. People claim that by following the book's advice, they feel better, their weight is better, blood pressure is decreased, and so on. And, of course, the testimonial implies that you should buy this book or adopt the method, sending all proceeds to the author.

But all the books can't be right—or right for everyone—as recommendations in one contradict another. Who's to testify which, if any, is best? With that note of caution, here's my testimonial, and it starts with the heart attack I mentioned earlier. After the attack, my weight loss was 10 percent in four months. Now over half a year later, the weight hasn't come back. It's gotten low enough that my wife thinks I should try to gain some pounds, but that's not happening. Measured by body mass index (BMI), I dropped from the slightly overweight category to a healthy weight. The BMI of a majority of Americans is above healthy, from overweight to obese, according to charts from the Centers for Disease Control. You can find your number at www.cdc.gov.

So what's my secret to weight loss and lower cholesterol? There really isn't one, and I've not taken to heart any of the books that claim to have an answer. I stepped up the exercise, although wasn't a couch potato before. I reduced meat and dairy, although I hadn't generally eaten large amounts of those before and had always watched salt carefully. Previously, I was not on a cardiac diet, mind you, but I ate more plant edibles than most, and I still had a heart attack. Now I've increased vegetables and fruits, replacing beef with beans, and I eat chickpeas and cabbage plus some raw carrots instead of chicken, cheese, and cookies. And I feel full with the veggies and only a little meat. It's not a difficult system.

Part III: Finances

Finances are a big part of retirement, and if your finances aren't in order, you'll have trouble helping others.

Do you

1. have a will (or trust) and other legal necessities?
2. know what you'll do for social security?
3. know what retirement plans you have (or don't have)?
4. know how much income you'll be getting?
5. know your likely expenses?
6. know your assets—cash, stocks and bonds, a house or condo, other?
7. know if you have adequate insurance?
8. have a plan for long-term health care?

Let's take each of these individually.

1. Will

If you don't have one, see a lawyer as soon as you can. If you have one, see that it's right for where you are now. An attorney is more than worth the cost of a review. And get his or her advice on such things as power of attorney for health care and a living will. Ask if you need an estate plan (even small estates can benefit) or perhaps a trust.

2. Social security

Have you made a decision? If you haven't, don't jump quickly—the choices are a real muddle. There are dozens of options, some of which can bring you extra thousands of dollars. In particular, if you have enough money for your current needs and longevity genes in your family, consider waiting until you're the maximum age of seventy and a half. By giving up current income, you'll get more per year, a valuable inflation hedge. Look at the Social Security website, www.ssa.gov, check out a book (*Personal Finance for Seniors for Dummies* has a good chapter), and talk with friends (but don't take everything they say as infallible advice—your situation is probably different).

Social Security is more than just retirement income; it provides disability and survivor benefits. Here we're interested in just retirement, and it's not simple. If you've already made a choice, then I hope you're set; if you haven't started, spend some time checking the options, because there are dozens. While you can start anytime you're over sixty-two, you can delay taking benefits until you're seventy. For every year you delay starting, you get 8 percent more, and that adds up. On the other hand, for every year you delay, you give up a year of benefits. It's a trade-off, and it's your call. Here are some more things to consider:

- If you're still working, the added income may reduce your benefits.
- If your spouse has benefits coming, you may want to take the benefits at different ages.
- If you have income in addition to social security, whether from savings or work, some of your benefits may be taxed.

Does it sound pretty involved? It is, so the best thing is to do your research. Check the Social Security Administration website (www.ssa.gov) and use their calculator at socialsecurity.gov/estimator. There are also books with information and advice, and you probably have friends who made their choice and will share their stories.

3. Retirement plans from your employer

Do you have one? If you do, is it an annuity, that is, it pays a fixed amount each year? This sounds good, but annuities have a way of shrinking. The dollar amount stays the same year after year, but the purchasing power goes down. That's inflation. Maybe your retirement is a 401(k) or 403(b) or 457, and you've got to decide if you should roll over into an IRA? This can be somewhat involved, but ask around and you may find you have colleagues who've gone through the process and have advice, or get a trustworthy financial advisor who can help you.

4. Income

Do you know how much income you'll be getting? Start with the retirement plan and Social Security. If you've got investments, your tax form should tell you what you need.

For income, probably last year's tax form will tell you most of what you need to know. Maybe you expect some additional income? Add it in.

Relating income and expense, when you were working, if you earned more than you spent, you were building cash, which was good. If you were spending more than you earned, your valuation was dropping, which didn't build toward retirement. Saving is no easy matter, but now, in retirement, you may have to draw down on your savings.

5. Expenses

Expenses are tougher to figure than income and a different list than you're used to. Lots of job-related costs, travel for one, will disappear, but others will pop up, such as coffee with a crew every Friday and travel.

Expenses are tougher, as they are scattered—food, transportation, and taxes are major, and an expensive vacation would stand out. Then there are the little expenses that can add up (more on that later). The key question is not just how much you make and spend, it's the difference between the two. Spending more than is coming in is a recipe for trouble.

Are you worried about outliving your savings? One alternative is an annuity, though you should look closely at the expenses involved. Instead, you might favor a charitable gift annuity. You give a chunk of money to a charity, and they give you a dependable income. That's the major benefit, but not the only one. You also get a tax write-off. Currently, a person aged seventy-five gets a rate of 5.8 percent per year. If you have $100,000 to give, that's an income of $5,800 a year, or almost $500 a month. There is a downside. When you die, the charity keeps any funds left over that they haven't paid out to you. If you are married, you can set up the charitable gift annuity in both your names, and a surviving spouse will continue to receive the income. However, a joint annuity pays less. There's another downside too; the payment doesn't increase as time goes by. As inflation eats away at your purchasing power, your fixed income will buy less. Want more details about charitable gift annuities? Check in with your favorite charity, and they'll be happy to explain things and give you all the assistance you need if you're willing to turn money over to them. The charity could be a hospital or medical charity, a religious or arts organization, or a museum.

A house is comfortable, and you're used to it, but sooner or later houses become a drag in effort and cost—there's regular upkeep of appliances, heating and cooling systems, roof, and yard, not to mention the expenses like utilities and real-estate taxes. Might you be better off in a condo or apartment or a retirement community? Investigate retirement living while you still have your health. Some retirement places have meal service, and most have activities. Many TV ads promote reverse mortgages, but I know several cases where people found out too late that they aren't such a good deal; avoid these if you can. There's a reason, actually several, that the industry doesn't have a good record.

We will discuss more later on how not to die broke and why owning some stock is good investment practice, as well as how to give money away.

6. Assets
Do you know how much you're worth, especially if you take away your house or condo? Figuring out what you're worth needn't be hard, and it is essential. How much money do you have in the bank (or credit union), whether checking, savings or CDs? How much do you have in stocks, bonds, and mutual funds? Some insurance policies have cash value, or maybe you've got a deferred annuity. Do you have a residence and funds in a retirement plan? What are they worth? Do you have significant debts, such as a mortgage or credit card balances?

One sheet of paper should do it, though if you want to be more detailed, your local library will have many books about totaling up your assets.

Knowing your situation is a big help. Say you've got a house and some money in the bank. As long as you have a rough idea of what the house is worth, it's fairly easy. But a house, even a valuable house, won't put food on the table. House expenses can be a drag on your finances. And how reliable is your income? Do you have enough to live on from a pension and Social

Security, or do you need to draw on savings? Maybe you've got an annuity. How much do you have in savings? Are those savings in bank accounts and certificates of deposit, or do you have equities, stocks, and bonds or mutual funds that hold stocks and bonds? What's the proportion between savings and equities? Without knowing how much you have, you can't know where you'll be.

After doing the figuring, do you think you're affluent, with lots of income and lots of investments, or at the other end, with a small income and not much saved up? We'll discuss assets further later in this section.

7. Insurance
If you have life insurance, you should look at not just what you have, but what you need, which may be nothing if you have no one dependent on you or have enough money for them.

If you are eligible for Medicare, and most retirees are, you have medical coverage, and it may be enough. Supplemental plans vary a lot, so don't get into one unless you know what it offers. A good rule of thumb is that insurance is for what you cannot afford. And it's not a free lunch—you have to pay for it, sometimes more than it's worth. Here is an example of a poor deal—one company offered a dental plan that cost well over $500 a year that capped benefits at $1,000.

8. Long-term health care
This one's troublesome, what with nursing home costs running upward of $5,000 a month even before medical expenses, and sometimes much more. Most people can't self-insure (have enough to pay those costs out of pocket), but look very closely before you buy a policy. You don't need a

policy that covers everything, as even in a nursing home, you'll have your regular income. Then you can't factor in how long you live and if you'll always be healthy. Average life expectancy when you've turned 65 is age 84.1, but who's average? You can guess at your health by looking at both your lifestyle and your family health history.

Donating—Another Look at Expenses

No matter what your net worth, are your expenses under control? A common mistake is spending accumulated funds or a nest egg without a projection to future needs. Even a millionaire can go broke. Another common mistake is thinking your income is what you can spend, regardless of whether that's $20,000 or $200,000, and spending to that level, forgetting taxes and the unexpected little things that add up. When you're in retirement and on a restricted income, you have to make your money last and watch expenses with added care. You can spot the big expenses easily. There's the federal tax bill come April every year, and there's real-estate tax. Buying a car stands out, as does a vacation or a major trip, especially when the credit card bill comes in. Other expenses add up, including frequent restaurant meals, even if not at pricey restaurants. A good term about how small expenses add up is the *latte effect*, also known as the *latte factor*—a phrase trademarked by financial author David Bach—which describes the small things consumers buy on a daily basis. Examples are coffee, cigarettes, and fast food, and of course a latte or a smoothie, that slowly but steadily erode income and bank accounts. Bach's suggestion was that this money spent on indulgences could instead be invested and saved for retirement or other goals. One way to see how you are doing is to track your expenses. Keep a notebook for a couple of weeks or a month and see where your money goes. Another approach is to skip something like your daily latte, put what you saved in a cup or a piggy bank, and see how much you have saved after a month. Imagine what you'd have over a year.

Here are some other thoughts about expenses in retirement:

- There are only two kinds of expenses, big ones and little ones, but if you spend little amounts regularly, it becomes big.
- Whatever you choose for parking your funds, especially investing, if it keeps you awake at night, it's not for you.
- Pay down credit card debt until you pay it off, and don't add more than is essential. Credit card debt is expensive—when you eliminate the interest and monthly charges, you'll have more for yourself.
- A reverse mortgage is a last resort and, even then, not a good one. Investigate very carefully.
- Perhaps you live where houses cost a lot. You could move to a smaller house, condo, or other arrangement. You could move to a less expensive area and use the difference for your living expenses.

Now that you've got yourself settled (or are working on it), what can you do that involves others? Of course you can donate to family, organizations, and causes.

You can give

- To your family. For grandchildren, start a college 529 plan or make a UGTM (Uniform Gift to Minor). For family, you can give $14,000 per year to each child, and a like amount to as many individuals as you want. They don't have to be family.
- To your religious affiliation.
- To charities, museums, and arts organizations. There are many good ones, but some others are close to scams. One group claiming to help veterans keeps ninety-five cents of each dollar it collects. The veterans get a nickel. And there are complete

scams, often with noble-sounding names, that often pop up after a disaster, such as a tornado, flood, or earthquake. Check the Better Business Bureau or Charity Navigator (charitynavigator.org) to separate out the ones that put your money to good use. Trustworthy examples include Doctors without Borders, which was on the ground in Africa during the Ebola outbreak, and the Salvation Army, which helps where needed without carrying high overhead.
- To your political affiliation or local candidates (this one doesn't get you a tax break, whereas the others do).
- To an advocacy group (some of these also don't get a tax break as they support candidates).

Besides donating dollars, you can be active. Your local church, synagogue, or mosque may need a volunteer treasurer, as may many charities and service organizations. If you are good with numbers, you can help without special training. You can also help others with their taxes. You don't need to be an accountant or tax expert. Check the website goladderup.org or see if AARP provides tax help in your town.

Maybe you're already overloaded with a combination of working, family, and volunteering. Donating money is a substitute for more volunteering. What's the cause that will get you to write a check? Do appeals for dread diseases, impoverished children, or veterans and police hit your hot button? Unfortunately, there are "charities" that do little for the cause they claim to represent, giving only pennies on the dollar. The rest goes into the pocket of the fund raiser.

A common trick is using a name similar to a reputable charity, ranging from attacking cancer to support for a local food bank. How do you tell the good from the bad? If it's local, such as a food bank, maybe you or friends have volunteered there and know it's effective. If you have a religious affiliation, you'll know how they spend their funds and whether the leaders are extravagant. Most leading organizations work on good causes, and most religions direct dollars and volunteers to good ends and deserve our support, though you probably know some bad examples that don't, like the TV preacher couple with solid gold faucets in their house or the sect leader with a fleet of Rolls Royces.

If the charities you know aren't local, how do you judge? Peter Singer, in his book *The Most Good You Can Do*, says there are almost a million charities in the United States that take in about $200 billion in donations, and that doesn't count religious contributions. Of the million, you can check some, including around seven thousand larger ones, at Charity Navigator (charitynavigator.org). The Better Business Bureau (www.bbb.org/charity-reviews) also is a place to look. Look for what percent is used for programs and what for administration and fund-raising. A good benchmark is at least 75 percent for programs. The Charity Navigator website has tips for donors for informed giving.

Singer also advocates "effective altruism," pointing out that your contribution is best directed where it will make a difference. His examples include preventing measles in poorer countries with vaccinations costing two dollars a shot and providing a mosquito net that would protect a child against the ravages, even death, from malaria. He prefers choosing to "do the most good" rather than what is most urgent. His reason? The most urgent likely already have funds flowing in from major donors.

And you thought giving money away would be easy.

Several charities we like are PrathamUSA, Doctors without Borders, and Echo (North Ft. Myers, Florida), all of which carry a four-star rating from

Charity Navigator and all with over 90 percent of contributions going to the organization's mission. Singer also mentions Oxfam, and we've worked with Habitat for Humanity and Heifer International.

After all that, let's discuss assets and investing in more detail.

How much did you come up with in item six above for your assets? Maybe a million?

A million dollars! It sounds like a lot, and is—but is it enough? Rodney Brooks, who writes for *USA Today*, has an e-book with that question as the title: *Is One Million Dollars Enough?* He's got a point. Say you've got a million dollars, you retired a week ago at age sixty-five, and you think you're set. Possibly not. If your million is in an "ultrasafe" savings account at your local bank and you take out $50,000 a year, by the time you're eighty-five, your million is gone. You're broke. But interest would give you more time, you say. True enough, though at current rock-bottom rates, you'd only get a few more months from the interest, and lots of folks live beyond eighty-five. Besides, in twenty years, inflation would hit your $50,000, just as most things now cost more than they did twenty years ago. You'd need more than that yearly amount to stay even. Of course there's Social Security, and maybe you've got a pension. Possibly you own a home that is paid off, which increases your valuation—though you can't buy groceries with a house. And maybe you decide to take "only" $40,000 a year, which gets you just past age ninety.

And whatever amount you have, what should you do with it? Turn it all into gold coins and put them under your mattress? You're missing what money can do. Say one person twenty years ago had taken the risk of investing in a mix of mostly stocks with some CDs, and averaged 6 percent compounded return. This is realistic, as stocks alone, given enough time, have averaged 7 percent. Compare the 6 percent investor with someone who invested "safely" in bonds at 3 percent. Sounds like for the risk, the stock investor got twice the yield. But what's missing? Taxes and inflation. Let's skip taxes for now and assume the funds are in a tax-sheltered account like an IRA, but include inflation at 2 percent, which is on the low side for the last two decades. Now what happens to yields? The real gain on the 6 percent drops to 4 percent, and 3 percent to 1 percent. Now the "risk premium" isn't twice as much, it's four times. And inflation is a financial fact.

While investing in equities gives you an edge, you have to stick with it, but psychology doesn't work in our favor. Let's say the proprietor of the local Widgets 4 U has a sale where every Widget is 50 percent off, and the sale is publicized via a full page ad in the local paper. Result? Almost no buyers. Then the owner takes out a half-page ad for a sale with everything double the price. This time he has to hire extra people to handle the rush. Does it seem unrealistic that double the cost brought in more customers? Of course, if it's Widgets or any other store product, but that's how folks behave toward stock—they buy more as prices rise. Don't believe that higher prices mean more buyers? In the 2008–09 and other market downturns, investors bailed out of stocks and mutual funds; when prices roared back, so did money pouring into funds, but it took a while, and some never got back, settling instead for "secure" yields of less than 1 percent. So did investors buy low, sell high? Nope, the opposite.

Earlier, we noted that even a million dollars can run out. Studies from the American Association of Individual Investors (AAII) show that being too conservative is riskier than taking some risk. If you're too conservative, you're at risk of running out of money. The journal of the American Association of Individual Investors from January 2016 has an article by Craig L. Israelsen about the risk of being "too safe." The example is someone with a conservative portfolio who keeps 25 percent in stock (including mutual funds) and 75 percent in fixed income (mostly bonds, 20 percent cash). If that individual withdraws at 7 percent per year and adjusts the cost of living by 5 percent every year, he or she has only a 2 percent chance of having money after thirty-five years. Of course, age sixty-five plus thirty-five gets you to age one hundred, but you'd be in trouble well short of that. What can you do to avoid going broke? Start with a lower withdrawal rate and don't increase your annual draw unless there is an emergency. With a 4 percent withdrawal and 3 percent annual cost of living adjustment, you have a 93 percent chance of lasting thirty-five years. Is there anything else you can do? Yes, have more stock: with a 65 percent stock, 35 percent in fixed income (mostly bonds, 10 percent cash) with a 4 percent withdrawal and 3 percent annual cost of living adjustment, you increase to 98 percent your chance of your funds lasting thirty-five years. Check aaii.com, Israelsen's website 7twelveportfolio.com, or books about financial planning for retirement.

Whether stocks or mutual funds, watching the stock market means knowing about indexes. There are several indexes that track stock prices. The oldest and best known of these is the Dow Jones, which has been around since 1896. I'm going to stick with that. Regardless of the index, the basics are the same—the prices of the indexes rise and fall because of the change in the value of the stocks in them. With enough time, months at a minimum, the ebb and flow of market valuations resembles a roller coaster, with its ups, downs, and curves. Looked at day to day, the roller coaster analogy fails us, as stock values can jump the track any day. While we notice the bumps, scary as they are, the long term is far more important than the short-term jolts. Let's look at some history. We don't need to view valuations back to the origin of the Dow or even note much about the Great Depression of the 1930s or post–WWII expansion.

Let's instead fast forward through the decades to the recession of 2008–09, when things looked glum for the world's economy and stocks tumbled the most since the Depression. From October 2007 to March 2009, the market dropped 57 percent. Pick any amount in stocks, whether directly held or in funds or retirement accounts, and values took a dive; you lost half the amount you were counting on. If you had $100,000 valuation in stock, in what seemed like no time, you were down closer to $50,000. Scary? Certainly! Too many panicked and sold, locking in their losses. But if you held on, your valuation eventually went back to $100,000 and beyond. And chances are you didn't have all of your bucks in an equities basket but had some in the bank and in bonds, damping the losses. Even if you weren't aware of it, if you had any retirement accounts, perhaps a 401(k), not all of that was in stock.

Not long after 2009, the trough and the panic were history as stocks rose, unsteadily at times, but eventually recouping the losses. If you weathered the financial storms of 2008 and 2009, are you better prepared mentally for another downturn? Things do turn around. Fast forward to a record high in May 2015, over 18,000 on the Dow Jones, and then the trend was down and you had to weather more volatility. How about a headline screaming "1,000 Point Plunge in Dow Stocks." That could have been the morning after August 24, 2015. The market was down over a thousand early on but finished the day down "only" 588, still the eighth biggest drop in history. The total drop in five days was over a thousand, or 5.6 percent. It's worse than a ride on a roller coaster that only plunges. When we see our assets melt away, what's our reaction? Panic? Sell everything and wait for a better day? How should we react? If you stay calm, cool, and collected, you'll probably see better days. August 26 and 27 were better days indeed, leaping almost 1,000. September and October were also wild, with lots of volatility, many a day of gains or plunges of over one hundred points.

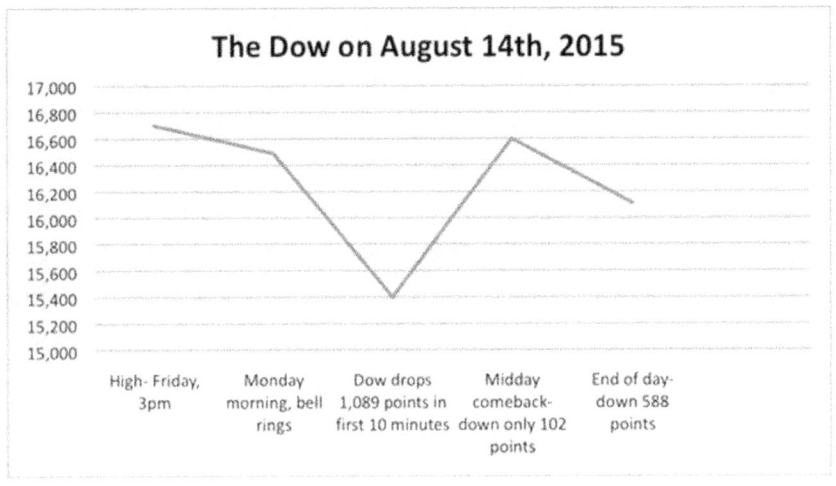

Data taken from CNN Money

What's the lesson? If you can manage to sit tight, you'll be all right. The newspaper columnists say stick it out; *stay the course* is a Vanguard watchword.

Spiritual

Cultivating a spiritual sense in your life is good for you. Eric Pfeiffer says churchgoers live fuller and longer lives. Experiencing spirituality doesn't have to mean being part of an organized religion, though for many, organized religion is the portal to the spiritual.

Unfortunately, through the ages, religious wars and fanaticism have tarnished religions, but there is good faith in most faiths. Expressions of help for the poor and unfortunate are ecumenical. Established religions promote good in word and deed. Does your religion have a golden rule or the equivalent?

Are revered sites prominent in your faith? Think of Jerusalem, important to Jews, Christians, and Muslims. Also for Muslims, there's Mecca, and for Hindus, Varanasi, Rameswaram, Mount Kailash, and many more.

Are pilgrimages and retreats, perhaps to the wilderness, a feature of your religion? Think of Lourdes and Mecca, think of Christ going alone or the Buddha under the Bodhi tree. In India, millions gather at the world's largest religious event, the Kumbh Mela. In New Mexico, there's the Sanctuario de Chimayo.

Most organized religions feature prayer or contemplation, whether alone or with a group. Being part of a religion, going to a service, joins you with other people, which itself is spiritual.

Most religions have a sacred expression or text. Think of the Bible, Torah, Koran, Ramayana, Bhagavad Gita, and of books about Buddhism or Zen. Rereading your choice or crossing over to an unfamiliar one may lead to spiritual insights, as might a reading of myths, including those from ancient Greece. While we know there's no Zeus on Mount Olympus hurling thunderbolts, there are psychological truths—spiritual truths—in these myths. And spiritual truths are evident in literature. Think of the insights in Shakespeare; think of the spiritual value of fine music and art.

Nature can be a portal to the spiritual, whether admiring the beauty of flowers or watching a sunset. Living day to day in a routine way, we may need a jolt to wake to a spiritual sense of nature.

Someone was on a safari in Africa and a fellow tourist, looking at the sky, asked, "What's that?" The answer was the Milky Way, meaning that the person asking the question had never known the wonders of the sky. And the Milky Way is just the plane of our galaxy. Light from the sun takes eight minutes to reach us, but light takes eighty thousand light years to cross our galaxy. The next closest galaxy, the Andromeda Galaxy, is visible to the unaided eye as a fuzzy patch. The light we see from that galaxy started on its way 2.5 million years ago. Beyond, visible only with powerful telescopes, lies the unimaginable spaciousness of the universe.

Around the earth, the northern lights dancing across the sky invoke a sense of awe. Back to earth, have you ever visited the Grand Canyon? Did your first view leave you awestruck? Watching deer in a meadow or walking through a meadow or a forest can take you out of yourself, calming your being (as long as the woods don't have too many mosquitoes), as can sitting by a tranquil pond or watching waves lap on a shore.

Meditation is an important part of some religions, but without being part of an organized religion, it can be spiritual. According to *Scientific American*, meditation exerts a positive influence.

Yoga, besides being good exercise, can have some of the same benefits as meditation. Forms of yoga do have a spiritual side as well as the physical movements, although in the United States, most of us think of yoga only for the physical.

Regardless of whether you would ever go on a pilgrimage or a spiritual journey, studies show that being part of a group, especially a religious group, is good for you and enables you to do good for others. Nicholas Kristof, in his book *A Path Appears,* says the most selfish thing you can do is help other people. Doing good is good for you. Being a volunteer is good for you.

CHAPTER 2

Finding Your Cause: Defining Your Values for Successful Philanthropy

Do you have a cause that you're dedicated to and passionate about? Is there an organization that you love and truly believe in their mission? Do you believe that you have a personal mission, and do you work toward accomplishing this through your actions?

If you answered yes to any of these questions, then congratulations! You've already accomplished the first step toward successful and meaningful philanthropy. Finding one's philanthropic purpose is an important accomplishment, and believe it or not this process is not as easy as it may seem. Individuals who have not had a mission-based career and are now approaching retirement may have never been granted the opportunity to express their values through philanthropy or give to a cause. You may not know where to start, and while trying to find a cause you're passionate about, you may discover that you care about *too many* things. There are so many important endeavors out there that need and deserve our support, and narrowing down your values can help you narrow down which causes you can support with conviction and heart.

Philanthropy is not only a way to give back to one's community, but also a chance to express your personal beliefs and values in an impactful way. A great first step toward being able to accomplish this is to first define what your values actually are, and this is not an easy process. A person's values and ideals are fluid—they change over time, are impacted by experiences and social influences, and are an ever-changing expression of you as a person. But where do your values come from? Values form the foundation of your life, and yet defining them is challenging, especially with so many outside influences telling us what to believe and how to feel, such as family, media, and pop culture.

For many, values come from religious teachings, and there are several clear guidelines to philanthropic giving set forth in religious texts. Let's explore some examples.

Christianity is the most widely practiced religion in the United States. The Bible states that one should give generously to those who are in need and share liberally with the poor. Particularly during Lent (for Catholics), Christians are to focus on the concept of almsgiving, which means donating money or goods to the poor and performing other acts of charity. Typically, almsgiving is seen as about 10 percent of one's income given back to the community. It also states that we may give our time unselfishly to our parents, spouse, and children.

The Jewish faith has a tradition of charity known as Tzedakah. Unlike other traditions, Tzedakah in the Jewish faith is absolutely a mandatory obligation and is not something done voluntarily. Excluded from many communities in early America, Jews had to take care of themselves and each other, which made charity and philanthropy part of their overall collective structure. Interestingly, Jewish charity comes in stages, or eight levels of giving (listed below, from lowest to highest form of giving), to guide one's giving with the highest form of charity as giving to another *before* they become impoverished (such as giving them a job, loan, or source of income).

Eight Levels of Jewish Charitable Giving

8. When donations are given grudgingly.
7. When one gives less than he should, but does so cheerfully.
6. When one gives directly to the poor upon being asked.
5. When one gives directly to the poor without being asked.
4. Donations when the recipient is aware of the donor's identity, but the donor still doesn't know the specific identity of the recipient.
3. Donations when the donor is aware to whom the charity is being given, but the recipient is unaware of the source.
2. Giving assistance in such a way that the giver and recipient are unknown to each other. Communal funds administered by responsible people are in this category.
1. The highest form of charity is to help sustain a person before they become impoverished by offering a substantial gift in a dignified manner, or by extending a suitable loan, or by helping them find employment or establish themselves in business so as to make it unnecessary for them to become dependent on others.

Similar to the Jewish tradition, Islam considers giving as a fundamental requirement within the faith. The word *Zakat* means "almsgiving or poor tax," and it is an absolute obligation. Zakat requires Muslims to give 2.5 percent of their annual assets, similar to the Christian concept of almsgiving. Alternatively, the concept of Sadaqah is voluntary charity that can be engaged in above and beyond the requirement of Zakat. In recent years, Muslim charities have been extremely open and transparent in their dealings, mostly due to greater scrutiny and prejudice after the 9/11 attacks.

The ideals of Buddhism are rooted in compassion, and this theme is weaved into all aspects of one's lifestyle rather than seen as a religious obligation (unlike many other religious practices). *Dana*, or generosity, connects individuals and community alike. Generosity, virtue, perseverance, and wisdom are all necessary for one to reach enlightenment, as Buddha did, and the quest to relieve suffering as part of a Buddhist practice is one of the oldest and most common roles of philanthropy.

While there was barely a Hindu presence in the United States before 1965, there are now more than 2.1 million Hindus living in the United States. In Hinduism, giving is an essential practice, especially on the part of the giver, as prosperity is said to come back onto the giver. There are four generalized rules for giving (*Dana*) in the Hindu tradition: give with faith, give with sensitivity, give with abundance, and give with the right understanding. It is also essential when engaging in Dana to give without expectations or strings attached to one's gift.

However, values do not have to come from religion. There are millions of people living full, meaningful lives without ethics derived from their religion. Religious affiliation does not define one's character or integrity, nor does it dictate which beliefs a person holds dear. In fact, the Dalai Lama himself has said, "I do not agree that ethics requires grounding in religious concepts or faith. Instead, I firmly believe that ethics can also emerge simply as a natural and rational response to our very humanity and our common human condition."

So where else can we look for values and where do we start? Many psychologists suggest looking back to one's childhood. Convictions forged in our youth can serve as a solid foundation for volunteerism and philanthropy with personal and social meaning. Look at your upbringing to try to identify influential people and experiences such as parents, trusted mentors/

adult influences, community, pivotal life events, and so on. What moments in your childhood and adolescence shaped what you think is important in life? How did they impact you? What opportunities might you have to impact someone else in the same manner?

Those people and experiences—both positive and negative—that made the biggest impression on us growing up never truly go away. Both good and bad experiences from childhood can shape our core beliefs about ourselves, others, and the world around us, and perhaps this exercise didn't help you define what values you want to emulate but can help eliminate those values you *don't* want (which is perhaps just as helpful). In fact, many people reject the values of their upbringing, and that is perfectly acceptable.

If you still feel lost, never fear. Another way to define your values is to look at other characters that impacted your life—the fictional ones. Many might dismiss this as a radical, somewhat far-reaching approach to adopting values, yet Luke Skywalker may have had more to do with a person's core beliefs than some family members, mentors, or religious figures. In many cases, science fiction shows us an advanced or Utopian universe where the problems that plague our world are obsolete. Take *Star Trek* for example. *Star Trek* displayed a multiracial and multiethnic cast and crew during the 1960s, when racial tensions were high and discriminatory practices were the norm.

Let's look at your favorite superhero as an example. What is it about him or her that you admire or would like to emulate? Besides flying faster than a speeding bullet or leaping tall buildings in a single bound, heroic figures show qualities worth adapting. Perhaps that character is brave and values social justice. Maybe he or she stands up for the weak and speaks out for those who are voiceless. Now let's switch gears and think of a beloved literary character. While reading *Harry Potter,* does Hermione Grainger's thirst and high regard for knowledge and academia make you want to support education? Did *Little Women*'s Jo March's smarts, gumption, and willingness to do anything for her family make you want to stand up for women's rights? These are all traits that can be easily expressed through philanthropy, advocacy, and volunteerism.

Another way to find your passion is to push your own buttons. Trying new things and observing one's response can be very telling to our own feelings, perhaps even when we were unaware of them. Watch the news, take in new information, read books, go to new places. Any and all of these things can elicit a response. A strong reaction to a social issue, role, or organization may be indicative that you've found something of value. That reaction may be one of strong compassion, thirst, empathy, love, or even intense rage—these are all good! That means you've hit on something that could be influential in your life.

After you think you've defined values that are a reflection of yourself, it's time to define what kind of service you'd like to engage in. You can give your time, talent, and treasure to a cause/organization, or perhaps you might engage in a mixture of all three. Above all, this service should be meaningful, impactful, and beneficial to the community *and* to you. That's right—philanthropy should make you feel good! There is nothing wrong with deriving pleasure from the act of giving. In fact, that's what makes us want to keep doing it. Lifelong philanthropy is mutually beneficial to both the giver and receiver.

Volunteerism is generally defined as the giving of one's time to an organization or cause. Regular volunteer service provides positive benefits to your health, social capital, and well-being. In fact, there is resounding psychological evidence that shows volunteers have motives apart from altruism. According to *Service-Learning and Psychology: Lessons from the Psychology of Volunteers' Motives*, a volunteer may seek to satisfy one of six main functions:

- Understanding—to learn, to gain a greater understanding of people, to practice skills and abilities
- Career—to enhance one's job or career prospects, to gain experience and contacts
- Values—to act upon important values such as humanitarian values, altruistic concerns, or desires to contribute to society.
- Social—to fit into important reference groups, to gain social approval, and to gain social capital
- Protective—to reduce feelings of guilt, to resolve or escape from one's personal problems
- Enhancement—to enhance one's self-worth and self-confidence and expand one's social network

Good volunteer service typically combines at least one of these functions, as we are more likely to become repeat volunteers if we reap multiple benefits from it apart from the "warm glow" of altruism.

Giving money to a cause or organization is another option you can engage in. We will go over nonprofits more in-depth in Chapter 5 to help guide you in choosing an organization that you feel confident will be a good steward of your monetary donation. Good financial giving comes from utilizing your heart *and* your head, and like other forms of giving, it should be mutually beneficial. If giving your money to an organization doesn't make you feel great, then it may be time to rethink your strategy!

Above all, charitable contributions of any nature (time, talent, treasure) should be joyfully given and received with gratitude. Charitable giving grants us the opportunity to express the deepest parts of ourselves and impact the world in a way that we choose. Defining one's values and figuring out which method of giving works best for *you* is the greatest thing you can do for the world, and it should not be taken lightly.

Andrea Groner's Story—Philanthropy and Self-Care through AmeriCorps

Some people find the inspiration to give at a young age and don't wait till they reach retirement. Andrea Groner found such inspiration to give when she was in her twenties, and her experiences will guide her through her life. By the time she retires, she will be an experienced Golden Giver. Her story is presented below.

Hurricane Katrina raged through New Orleans in August 2005 when I was eighteen years old. I had just graduated high school and was poised to move to New York within the month to attend Manhattan School of Music, a top-tier music conservatory, to study oboe performance. I had always been musically inclined and had grown up in a household where the arts were nurtured and encouraged. My mother is a violinist, my father is a conductor, and I was an oboist and singer; with just a little more imagination, we could have given the Von Trapp family a run for their money.

I remember clearly the images on CNN of the thousands of scared, tired faces of those injured or displaced by the storm. The stories of people who lost everything in a moment and had no idea how to begin rebuilding their lives from the ground up seemed to stick with me for weeks afterward. I would put off practicing my orchestral excerpts in lieu of watching Anderson Cooper expose the hard truth about the inadequacies of recovery efforts and I remember thinking, "That's where I belong." Every part of my heart wanted to drop everything and go help in any way that I could, but the conservatory waited for no one. It was highly competitive to attend Manhattan School of Music (MSM), and I could not risk my skills depleting. Ultimately, I moved as scheduled to New York City to begin a career as a classical musician.

After two years of work at MSM, I came to the sobering realization that while music was something I had always excelled at, it was not something that I had a burning passion for. I saw my classmates light up when talking about their craft, I saw contentment on their faces after six hours in a dingy practice room, and I saw a fire in their eyes to become the best players possible.

They felt comfortable in an institution where they focused on *only* music, while I, on the other hand, found it stifling. I felt as though I was letting some opportunity slip through my fingers, an opportunity to explore other passions and paths that could lead me to being my fully realized self.

I knew that I had to make a change in my life, so I made the choice to explore volunteer service gap years with AmeriCorps. On Christmas Day in 2009, I found out that I had been accepted to the National Civilian Community Corps (NCCC), a branch of AmeriCorps for young adults ages eighteen to twenty-four. We were all thrilled; I was diving into something new and scary head-first, and I felt incredible. By February, I had relocated to Perry Point, Maryland, and was surrounded by a more diverse and eclectic group of people than I had ever encountered before. In one house or team, it was the norm to have people of several different backgrounds, ethnicities, faiths, and political views.

We lived in houses on the VA hospital campus, where we went through several weeks of training before eventually getting placed in teams of eight to ten individuals, with one team leader. Those teams were the people you'd spend every minute with for the next ten months of your life, traveling from place to place around the country in a large "Mystery Machine"–style van to serve nonprofit organizations for eight to ten weeks at a time before returning to Perry Point between projects. NCCC allowed me to travel around the country to cities I never thought I'd see and work on projects I never thought I'd be capable of. The range of diversified skills that are acquired in NCCC is absolutely staggering.

Our first project was out of Lake Charles, Louisiana, working for Habitat for Humanity. Habitat, if you are not familiar with the organization, builds homes for low-income individuals. We built houses from the ground up and learned construction skills that have come in handy to this day when renovating my own living spaces throughout my life. Our team was even featured in the local paper for the work we did, and for that I am eternally grateful.

The next project I engaged in was in Baltimore, Maryland, with the Samaritan Women. This organization is near and dear to my heart, as the executive staff was made up of some of the kindest and most compassionate people I have ever met. Baltimore is a surprisingly rough town—there is a very high crime rate, and it is a hot zone for human trafficking activity. The Samaritan Women is a Christian organization that provides care to survivors of abuse and human trafficking. They help fund their mission with a multiple-acre organic farm, which our NCCC team planted and tended. I learned more about gardening from them than I ever had before, and we got to literally see the "fruits of our labor." We stayed all together in a farm house and enjoyed family-style dinners with the staff; we truly became close during our time there. One day, I was asked to remove some poison ivy from a tree on the property. I am immune to poison ivy, as is everyone in my family, so I was the natural choice. I was not careful and fell out of the tree, breaking my left wrist upon impact. I felt terrible that I would be unable to give full effort to them, but the whole team and leaders responded with unwavering support. We all took care of one another and took great pride in our work. Because I have always thought of myself as (and had a reputation as) an "indoor girl," working in a garden every day was incredibly transformative and impactful for me.

Next, we ventured to Camden, New Jersey. Camden is a dangerous town to say the least; it has one of the highest crime rates in the country. However, it also has some of the biggest "food deserts" in the nation. Food deserts are areas in which there is lack of access to fresh, affordable produce without cars or transportation. Without access to these fresh foods, those in low-income brackets or those without transportation are forced to eat fast food or convenience store food, which negatively impacts their overall health. Our team worked with the Camden Children's Garden to combat this issue. The Camden Children's Garden helps to educate youth in nutrition and healthy choices while offering tours of whimsical gardens full of fruits, vegetables, and exotic flowers. They also have rides, a butterfly garden, and trails (that our team would regularly take full advantage of for "fun breaks"), as well as large statues of animals and literary figures, my favorite of which was a giant Edgar Allan Poe that I would regularly talk to when no one else was nearby. We participated in youth nutrition education and tended to their vast gardens most of our days.

The Camden Children's Garden also maintained several urban gardens around town to combat these food deserts and provide the locals with fresh organic produce. We tended to these gardens regularly as well and talked with the locals about the changes in their eating habits and cooking. We also worked closely with the New Jersey Tree Foundation, an organization that quickly became one of our favorites to do weekend volunteer work with. They planted trees all over Camden, which strengthened their community by instilling a sense of pride in their surroundings. Having more foliage around was also a crime deterrent and helped to beautify the neighborhoods. Our time in Camden really helped us link social problems with community-wide solutions and taught us how governments and nonprofits collaborate together to address social issues when one branch is battling issues such as lack of funding or a plethora of red tape.

Our team took a mini-spike (*spike* is the term that NCCC uses for nonprofit assignments) in Washington, DC, for about two weeks, working with Greater DC Cares. We did a number of projects for them, the most awe-inspiring of which was renovating a middle school. While this project seemed basic, we had no idea our lives were about to change. Once we were settled in DC, our team leader asked us for our Social Security numbers. This seemed like a strange request, as they'd never needed these before and were reluctant to disclose why they were required.

Several days later, on the night before our service project taking place on September 11, we were informed that President Obama would be stopping by the school we were working on for a visit. We were floored. President Obama stopped by the school and greeted everyone in the room with a charisma and energy that I had never seen before. He naturally won over everyone in the room and seemed genuinely interested in everything we had to say. We eventually got a few minutes with him to talk and share our experiences with him, and then we posed for a group picture with him, which is being used for AmeriCorps projects all over the country to this day.

While NCCC provided me some of the best times of my life, it did not come without disadvantages. NCCC was a lot more militarized and structured than I had anticipated.

Everyone wore regulation uniforms of a gray T-shirt, khaki pants, black belt, and work boots, all of which were unisex and distinctly unflattering. Teams endured military-style physical training and PT Tests every few weeks to make sure we kept up our stamina. There was no alcohol allowed in living quarters, nor was "cohabitating" with members of the opposite sex allowed. The consequences for breaking these rules were severe, and the punishments process was highly controlled by team leaders—every conflict, every fight among team members (of which there were many), and every disagreement was documented and handled according to a specific conflict-resolution process. Teams were often times so different, so diverse, with lots of conflicting personalities and opinions within such tight quarters—arguments were bound to happen. Also, the age parameters on the team often added to the tension. While many team members were fresh out of high school and used to a regimented environment, there were others (like myself) who had already established independent lives with housing of their own where they were free to make their own decisions apart from a parental authority figure. Having the freedom to control your life and choices taken away from you contributes greatly to feelings of resentment and anxiety, which was definitely a distraction from the good work we were able to accomplish.

For me, the best part of my participation in AmeriCorps NCCC was the fact that I finally got to New Orleans during our third spike, the beloved city that had inspired my career in service. We worked for an organization (let's call them Organization X) that was still rebuilding homes for victims of Hurricane Katrina five years after the storm hit. I had no idea that there was so much work still to be done, and I was happier than ever to assist. Given my previous work experience, I made my case to the founder of the organization and she promptly put me into a position in the office to assist with their event marking the fifth anniversary of Katrina. They had never had a member of NCCC that was qualified to work in their offices, so it was an experiment that they were eager to try.

After just a few weeks, upper management at Organization X made it clear that they wanted me to stick around and encouraged me to graduate early from NCCC to come work for them through AmeriCorps State (another branch of AmeriCorps). All it would take to do this was to work sixty to eighty hour weeks in order to finish the program early—which, looking back, may have been the biggest feat of all. At the time, we were on our last project in Wells, Maine, working with the Wells National Estuarine Research Reserve. It was our job to maintain their trails by removing invasive plant species, building trails, and restructuring habitats for the endangered New England cottontail rabbit. I was determined to go above and beyond their expectations, fueled by an obscene number of lobster rolls that we consumed daily. I had always been determined but had never felt the drive to accomplish something more in my life than getting to New Orleans. I encourage anyone to give an early-twenties Type-A kid with a dream a challenge in stamina—then stand back and watch him or her exceed all your expectations. In the end, I graduated from NCCC early and was able to travel right away to New Orleans, the place of my daydreams.

New Orleans is where my work truly started and where I learned the greatest lesson of all about service—you must practice self-care if you hope to take care of others. I quickly made friends within Organization X and established myself as a professional force. After a couple of weeks, Jim (his name has been changed to protect his identity) the CEO approached me and informed me that I was being considered for a new role—as his executive assistant. I was eager to ingratiate myself to him, as he was clearly successful at his job and was a master relationship-builder in the New Orleans community. With a background in law, he knew how to spin any situation in his favor with his natural charisma and could turn a golf outing into a fifty thousand dollar donation. He was impressive, direct, and extremely intimidating. Naturally, I jumped at the opportunity to advance my professional career and establish myself as he had. I quickly learned that he would be the toughest boss that I'd ever work for and that my time in New Orleans would be challenging both personally and professionally.

I had a wonderful group of friends that provided comfort for me, and I lived with a loving family that was warm and welcoming. We were able to secure several members of Obama's campaign staff to come in and instruct our team on how to recruit more volunteers and funding into our organization. We even had Madeline Albright take an interest in our work; she stopped by the office to check it out and commented happily on how the office was made of "a lot of strong women," which was true, as the staff was about 85 percent women at the time. We were enamored with her, and she provided us with a much-needed boost in confidence and stamina.

Organization X allowed me to gain new skills that I still use today as a nonprofit professional—I was able to assist and plan fundraisers that resulted in over one million dollars in revenue, I got a plethora of experience dealing with nonprofit governing boards, arranged volunteer activities, learned about the nature of disaster recovery and how nonprofits fulfill a desperately needed role when government aid fails to address the needs of its people. When all is said and done, I would do it all over again, because the benefits to my professional skill set far outweighed the stress.

With that being said, I want to talk a little more about the subject of philanthropy and self-care. My experience can serve as a cautionary tale to any aspiring nonprofit professional (or eager volunteer) who wants to make a difference but puts himself or herself secondary to the needs of the cause or organization.

A concept of "saintly givers" was introduced to me at school—early American settlers (mostly Catholic missionaries) who would literally take care of people until they starved to death or their health deteriorated. They put all of their earthly needs aside in order to care for others, even to the point of extreme self-sacrifice. We exalt these people for their altruism, but I can't help but wonder—is this the best way to be of service?

There is a theory put forth by Dwight Burlingame, of the IU Lilly Family School of Philanthropy, that philanthropic acts can be placed on a scale of egoism and altruism. Some philanthropy is entirely altruistic—where the giver receives absolutely no benefit, not even the "warm glow" of giving.

Alternatively, some philanthropy is done strategically and egoistically. Perhaps to get someone's name on a building, to increase a company/individual's image or to create a program that will ultimately be self-serving. But then the question arises: *should* philanthropy be entirely altruistic?

If we are to accept pure altruism as the norm, where the giver receives no benefits, is this truly the best way to encourage continual giving? Animals are programmed to repeat actions that make us feel good, otherwise we'd starve to death and never procreate. If the act of giving to others is not pleasurable, we are unlikely to engage in it again. Furthermore, it creates an undesirable relationship with the recipient and deems them a "charity case," which closes off that relationship to any further giving opportunities.

We exalt altruism as a society, and this is seen in many places, most often in the criticisms of nonprofit organizations. Media, donors, and supporters feel free to chastise a nonprofit CEO for making more money than they feel he or she should or paying staff "too much"—and then wonder why the nonprofit sector isn't able to recruit the best and the brightest minds into their organizational cause. Executives at for-profit companies who manage thousands of people and bring in millions of dollars in funding are praised and elevated as "self-starters" who are living the American dream. Then, a nonprofit leader who manages the same number of people and brings in the same level of funding is rebuked for driving a car that is "too fancy." Ultimately, it is the concept of altruism that allows people to go on believing the nonprofit sector should be making miracles out of nothing.

Giving, philanthropy, and volunteerism should be from the heart and joyfully given, but never at your own expense. This will contribute to feelings of negativity, resentment, and eventual burnout, which will not help yourself (or others) in the long run. This is a lesson that I had to learn the hard way through hours of strife mixed in with hours of pure joy from seeing the faces of those that I impacted. The bottom line is that you *can* help others immensely, but it should never subtract from your own well-being or change who you are.

There is a certain freedom that accompanies giving 100 percent of yourself over to a cause. To throw all of your time, efforts, funds, and future into an organization you believe in makes you feel purposeful. However, we need to be sure that we are still putting ourselves first and that we are living a life that makes us happy before we can offer anything of substance to others. I look back on my time with AmeriCorps as a period in my life that was hard, fulfilling, and necessary. Some of the best and worst times of my life came with volunteer service, and I would do it again in a heartbeat. I learned more about the nature of nonprofit organizations, the nature of people and the nature of myself under pressure than in any other period in my life, and for that I will always be grateful.

I encourage any youth looking for something useful and fun to do with ten months of their life to join AmeriCorps. It will challenge you mentally, emotionally, and physically to accomplish things you never dreamed you could do. It will also result in some of the best, most enduring friendships of your life. Sacrificing your blood, sweat, and tears (in many cases that is literal) together creates a bond with one another that is impossible to shake. I consider my AmeriCorps friends some of the very dearest to me, and even though our bodies are in different locations, our hearts will always be together in service.

I will leave off with the AmeriCorps pledge, as it is the perfect representation of the service that fuels progress in this country and keeps hearts beating strong all over the world.

I will get things done for America—to make our people safer, smarter, and healthier. I will bring Americans together to strengthen our communities. Faced with apathy, I will take action. Faced with conflict, I will seek common ground. Faced with adversity, I will persevere. I will carry this commitment with me this year and beyond. I am an AmeriCorps member, and I will get things done

Photo 1: Andrea with Anderson Cooper at a CNN Broadcast from "Musicians Village," Habitat for Humanity, 2010. Photo 2: A Greater DC Cares service project on September 11, 2010, with President Barack Obama.

CHAPTER 3

Giving Locally

We are always looking for human connections, and the well-known saying "No man is an island" is very true. We feel good when we can help anyone, and a smile or a thank you warms our heart. All our religions have guidelines to help others through charity and selfless giving. Most Christian denominations believe in giving 10 percent of income to help the community, and other religions like Hinduism and Muslim have traditions for giving to deserving persons without fanfare or recognition, as a matter of one's duty. However, giving money (treasure) is only one way of giving; you can share your talents with someone in need or give your time to help others—the three Ts.

Americans are the most generous people on earth. We contribute more than $350 billion in charitable contributions every year and give time to help our neighbors, our community, and the elders in our household. Many young people start giving in schools to projects around the world, and this develops the philanthropic spirit in young people. We have read-a-thons, walk-a-thons, marathons, and many other community events that we organize to raise money for the various causes that Americans support. The chart below shows where US charitable dollars are going.

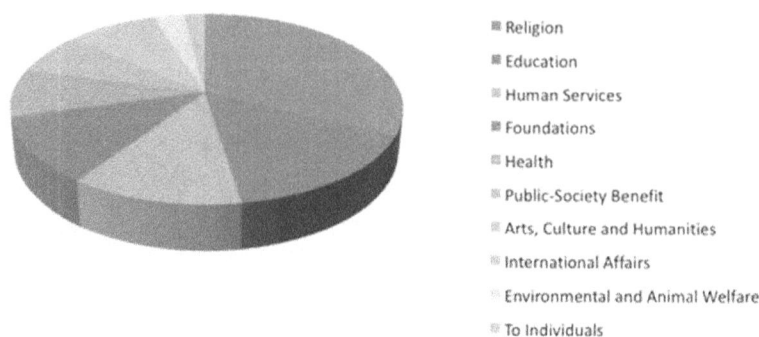

2015 Charitable Contributions

- Religion
- Education
- Human Services
- Foundations
- Health
- Public-Society Benefit
- Arts, Culture and Humanities
- International Affairs
- Environmental and Animal Welfare
- To Individuals

Source: Giving USA Report 2015

Around the world, people are doing things for their neighbors and communities. The ways of giving are as varied as the needs of the communities and the interests of the volunteers and cultures. However, the pleasure of helping others is universal and world-wide; giving is in trillions of dollars. In many countries, people retire at age sixty, and many of them are giving back. These retirees find purpose in their lives through taking care of their communities' needs through feeding the poor, education, and being involved in established charitable organizations.

There are many ways to help your local community. The main ways to give can be broadly broken down into the following categories:

- environmental cleanup or beautification
- education, including tutoring/mentoring
- joining a service organization like Lions Club or Rotary Club
- health care
- citizen activism/political advocacy
- food pantries

- legal services
- music/arts organizations
- helping the homeless
- helping with job training or entrepreneurial development

Environmental Projects

Environmental opportunities abound in our local communities. From cleaning our parks, rivers, and lakes to serving on environmental commissions set up by government officials, the opportunities for changing our community for the better are plentiful. This kind of effort also sets a great example for our children, who can help along with us to clean our local parks. On Earth Day every year, communities provide opportunities for young and old alike to get involved in projects to improve our environment. Park districts in all communities organize spring cleanup days, environmental awareness tours for young people, and other opportunities for seniors to impart knowledge to young folks and clean up our parks and lakes.

If you're an animal lover, linking up with an animal shelter might suit you perfectly, and there's almost always a need for volunteers. No special knowledge is necessary to get you on your way, and you can even specialize. My phone book lists collie rescue and I've seen similar mention for greyhounds. Check your phone book or see if a local branch of the humane society would match your interests. Dogs and cats are the standard, often abandoned animals, but wildlife such as birds with broken wings need care too. One note of caution: be sure that any facility you help with matches your viewpoint. Perhaps you insist on a no-kill policy, and the shelter doesn't, leaving you unnerved and frustrated. If you live near a zoo, you might join forces. Most have memberships that give you special privileges, and some have volunteer slots. As any zoo is expensive to operate, support including donations is vital, and you will learn more about the animals than you would from a routine visit. There are even special sanctuaries for wolves and exotic animals such as large cats.

Coauthor Keith Olson cleaning up the Great Western Prairie in Elmhurst, Illinois. Photo by Daniel White, Daily Herald.

The outdoors is a great place to volunteer. My pet project is a natural area, specifically a prairie, my bit of wildness right in a suburb in Illinois. Why a prairie? Partly because it's here, partly because the prairie was the original landscape of much of central North America. Prairies were a dominant landscape, from patches as far east as Pennsylvania to the Rocky Mountains and occasionally beyond, from the Gulf of Mexico to the prairie provinces of Canada. And what do volunteers do? They work to keep out invasive plants, just as you would work to keep the weeds out of your own lawn and garden, and they keep the area clean. For this effort, no special skill is needed, just a willingness to get dirty, and ages from well-supervised preschoolers to folks in their eighties can participate. To do something similar, a prairie isn't essential—a woodland, marsh, or dune will do nicely. Maybe you're near a park with a natural area or a nature center that relies on volunteers. Most of the units of the National Park System (nps.gov), the Forest Service, and many state parks and agencies welcome volunteers.

What's in it for you? Besides doing good work, you get outside, exercise, learn something new, and make new friends. And you could connect with one or more of the raft of organizations doing their thing for the environment. Nationally, the list is long—the Sierra Club, the Audubon Society, the National Wildlife Federation, Ducks Unlimited, the National Parks Association, the League of Conservation Voters, the Nature Conservancy, and so on. Do a web search for any of them, and you'll find others that may suit your interest. While their mission statements vary, they have advocacy at their core but carry it out in different ways. The Sierra Club, despite carrying the name of a California mountain range, has local chapters, sponsors a range of outings, and is politically active, even endorsing candidates. That means if you donate to the Club, you can't claim the donation on your taxes, but the Club also has a foundation with tax deductible status. Many, but not all, of the other organizations listed are tax exempt and usually operate both locally as well as nationally. Get on a mailing list for any of them and you'll quickly find out. You may be able to participate in an advisory group about the environment. I served on an environmental commission for the county where I live for over a decade. Although the commission had no authority to decide issues, it was a great springboard for viewpoints and information for the county board and administrators.

If nature's not your thing, have you ever noticed those signs along the highway that say "This section kept clean by…"? That could be you, and you could multiply your efforts by gathering the assistance of a business, service group, or organization. Besides keeping the area clean, you and the participants bond, and the group or business gets positive notice.

Education

Interactions between seniors and young people in school or college can be very rewarding, transferring the knowledge and experience accumulated over a lifetime of work to young people who are in school, in training, or have just joined a company. There are many opportunities in cities and rural communities to tutor/mentor high school children. My most rewarding experience in Chicago has been tutoring high school children and adults through the DuPage Literacy Center. I have also served as their mentor, guiding them in their career choices and spending weekends with them occasionally. I was assigned a tenth grade student who was failing her math and science courses. She said, "I hate math and science, but love reading and writing." I told her that nothing is difficult if you work at it and focused on teaching her math and physics. With a lot of encouragement, and diligent work for just two hours a week, I helped her change her grades to B and B+ in math and physics." When she was admitted to college, the first member of her family to do so, "that was a very proud moment for her and for me."

DuPage Literacy Center helps immigrants learn English and find jobs in Chicago. I (Rajaram) had the opportunity to work with an immigrant from Burundi who was caught in the civil war in the country. Working with him on his English skills, job search, and adjustment to life in the United States was a nice challenge. Within a few months of starting the tutoring program, he got a good job at a manufacturing company. With improvement in spoken English and reading and writing, he became a useful member of the Chicago community. It was good to see him settle in Chicago and take care of his family. All it took was two hours once a week to change the life of an immigrant.

There are plenty of organizations and after-school programs looking for volunteers. The seniors have the opportunity to interact with a young person and have a positive influence on his or her life. Many broken families can use this assistance, and it will address many of the social ills in our cities. Providing guidance and improving a young person's life is very rewarding, and I recommend it to all who are reading this book.

Service Organizations

America and countries around the world have great service organizations that cater to the needy in our communities. Some organizations build capacity in our youth, others inculcate the spirit of service, and all of them serve the unmet needs that the government alone cannot provide for. These organizations provide people an opportunity to volunteer and help their fellow citizens. Governments encourage such activities by exempting these organizations from the payment of taxes, since they are filling the gaps that the government leaves in society. Some organizations focus only on local needs, while others like the Lions Clubs and Rotary Clubs provide their services in countries around the world.

Lions Clubs International

This organization was started in 1917 by a few businessmen in Chicago who wanted to help their fellow citizens. Under the leadership of Melvin Jones, the Lions Clubs grew all over the United States, Canada, and internationally. In 2016, Lions Clubs International had clubs in 210 countries and did humanitarian work worldwide, with the help of 1.3 million members. The clubs are independent but operate under the universal motto of "We Serve." Local clubs have 25 to 150 members, and they focus on serving the local needs in the community. As you will read in chapter 8, some clubs get involved in international activities using the assistance of the Lions Clubs International Foundation (www.lcif.org). Clubs work together for the benefit of the poor in various communities, and the span of their service activities varies from club to club. Although *Service to the Blind and Prevention and Treatment of Eye Diseases* has been the main goal of Lions Clubs International since Helen Keller challenged them with this task in 1925, the club performs many charitable activities:

- Training youth in leadership and service—Leo Clubs around the world inculcate the spirit of service in children aged eleven to fifteen
- Helping hungry people in the community, a partnership with the Global Food Banking Network of Chicago
- Helping the disabled through assisting with sports for the visually handicapped
- Vaccinating against measles in association with the Gates Foundation
- Addressing the needs of the local community where the club is located

Lions Clubs offer a great way for you to be involved in serving your community, and as you retire, you can do more for your club and the causes your club is serving. The camaraderie of other club members while you serve your community is another big benefit of belonging to a Lions Club. The range of services offered and the ways to raise money to provide these services are endless, and it is a nice challenge to have in life. Monthly meetings are held to plan the events and execute them for the community.

Rotary International

The Rotary Club was started by a Chicago businessman, Paul Harris, in 1905, and now has a presence in more than two hundred countries around the world. Rotary Clubs operate in a similar way to Lions Clubs. Although their rules and the causes they serve are different, service to fellow human beings is the hallmark of both Lions and Rotarians. The projects in which they are involved vary from small water projects in Africa, India, and many other countries to the eradication of polio worldwide. I know many Rotarians who give their time, talent, and treasure all through the year addressing the problems in small communities within the United States to projects that impact the welfare of people around the world.

Junior Chamber International

The Junior Chamber International (or JCI) is a nonprofit headquartered in Coral Gables, Florida, that is composed of young people between the ages of eighteen and forty. It was founded in 1915 in St. Louis and has more than 170,000 members worldwide in more than 124 countries. JCI seeks to gather active citizens to develop skills and understanding to participate in efforts toward international cooperation and a more peaceful society. While there are national chapters, most work happens at the grassroots level in local towns. JCI members analyze challenges within their communities and work with partners to conduct projects that reach solutions. They then evaluate their results to make sure they can be sustained for long periods of time. Jaycees International Foundation is JCI's sister foundation that funds projects of JCI members to enable them to engage in meaningful service projects.

Kiwanis International

Kiwanis International was founded in Detroit, also in 1915, and is headquartered in Indianapolis, Indiana. Kiwanis is also a global agency; it can be found in more than eighty nations with more than six hundred thousand members. Kiwanis specifically serves the needs of children through the local service projects and fund-raising efforts of its members. According to their website (Kiwanis.org), club members host about 150,000 service projects and complete 18.5 million service hours per year. They raise about $100 million a year to support causes at a grassroots level as well as to support the Kiwanis Children's Fund (a foundation similar to JCI's), which is used to fund Kiwanis youth programs, provide scholarships, and give grants to organizations.

Knights of Columbus

The Knights of Columbus is one of the oldest service organizations in America. In the late eighteen hundreds, there was a large boom in "mutual benefit" organizations such as sororities and fraternal organizations (more on that in chapter 5). Knights of Columbus is one such organization. Founded in 1882 in New Haven, Connecticut, Knights of Columbus is one of the oldest and largest fraternal organizations in the world. It originally began as an insurance company (before it was privatized) and quickly grew into a volunteer haven. As it is a fraternal organization, only men can be members (sorry, ladies) and it is based in Catholicism. Their website states that their "principal work involves helping others in need," through volunteer projects and monetary charitable giving.

Shriners International

The Shriners was established in 1870 and is headquartered in Tampa, Florida. While it is associated with Freemasonry, it is considered an "appendant body." The Shriners are another fraternity, with about 350,000 members in approximately ten countries. The Shriners are most known for the Shriners Children's Hospitals, which provide excellent services to ill children. They are also known for their trademark red fez hats that they wear, which represents the Arabian theme that they were founded on. Shriners are also committed to public service and engage in community service projects at the local level.

Health Care

Hospitals in the United States require volunteers for all aspects of care, from administrative duties to patient care. Many seniors enjoy giving their time to help the people in hospitals. In addition, the nursing care and assisted living industry is growing in the United States, and there will be need for volunteers to keep them running well while minimizing costs. The human interactions and the sense of accomplishment are great in volunteering for helping people in hospitals or other locations. In the twenty-first century, children are too busy to spend time with their parents when they are in declining health, and volunteers can fill this gap well.

There are many ways to volunteer in hospitals, including

- in the gift shop;
- visiting patients during their stay;
- in the office; and
- many other tasks which are not fully staffed.

Patients in wheelchairs often need to be moved. If you enjoy the human contact, talking to the patients, their families, and hospital staff can be very rewarding. There are lots of other seemingly small but necessary things, like helping with admissions, assisting the administrative staff, and working in the gift shop. Volunteers are essential and help reduce the cost of health care or make it better.

And there's advocacy for attention to health issues. Pick a disease, and there's almost certainly an organization that focuses on that illness. Besides dollar contributions, they too often welcome volunteers for many of the same sorts of things as political outfits, from stuffing envelopes to advocacy. If you've been personally affected by a disease, even as a bystander, you may know of one. If not, the phone book, the Internet, or a library help desk can get you going.

Youth Services

One of the most meaningful volunteer experiences at any age of life is to help a child achieve his or her full potential. There are many ways to help children, as trusted and reliable adults are always needed to lend their time to the development of a child. No matter his or her background, each child deserves caring adults that he or she can depend on; you can be that person for a child in a number of ways:

- Become a mentor. There are several organizations that pair children with mentors in order to improve the outcomes of children (such as avoidance of risky behaviors, greater confidence, higher aspirations, higher graduation rates, and educational success). One of the largest and most trusted organizations in this area is Big Brothers Big Sisters. They are present in nearly every major city and are proven to improve outcomes for children and families in their program. They pair children facing adversity (Littles, as they are called) with a trusted adult (a Big) to spend time with one another and help change their lives for the better. These mentoring relationships are professionally supported by a team of trained experts who monitor the health of the match regularly through calls, meetings, and agency-sponsored activities. Prospective Bigs go through a background check and a vigorous interview process (after all, one can never be too thorough when it comes to the safety of children) and are then paired with a Little within the same area to ease transportation strains. Once matched, they go through training and are continuously supported and coached by Big Brothers Big Sisters staff. To learn more about BBBS, go to www.bbbsa.org and find a branch near you to become a Big.

- Tutor at an after-school program. Assisting kids with their homework is something that is vital for educational success. Perhaps they're living in a single-parent household where their mother or father is working to support their livelihoods—and sometimes helping kids with homework is less important than earning money for them to survive. This is where you come in! Tutor volunteers can serve at homeless shelters, School on Wheels, Learning Centers, or at actual schools. Tutored children can see up to three times more growth in their math and reading scores than other children—all from volunteering just a few times a week for an hour or so. With new technologies being adapted in educational strategy every day, sometimes volunteers experience just as much education as the children do. Focused attention is one of the greatest gifts you can give to students!

Citizen Activism/Political Advocacy

In a democracy, dynamism and effectiveness is possible only if citizens participate actively in the government. The rate of political participation has been declining in the United States, with voter participation in national presidential elections around 50 percent and for local elections falling to around 30 percent. This causes cynicism and lack of faith in political institutions like the US Congress, state legislatures and city councils. Several citizen advocacy organizations are actively seeking accountability in government and helping ordinary, undervalued citizens participate in the political process. The League of Women Voters takes an active part in local, state, and federal elections, conducting candidate forums so voters know about the issues and how the candidates promise to tackle these issues. In Illinois, a young lawyer named Theresa Amato started the Citizen Advocacy Center (CAC) in 1993 to encourage citizen participation in the political process and help citizens claim their rights as citizens. Porus Dababhoy's inspirational story is provided in chapter 8.

Food Banks

Food is a basic necessity, and many in the United States and around the world go hungry for lack of food or eat food that is not nutritious. This impacts health and productivity and is a problem that is being solved by governments and civic groups. It is very satisfying to help a person who is hungry, and there are many opportunities in the United States to help the hungry:

1. Work as a volunteer in a local food pantry, distributing donated food to the hungry.
2. Donate food to the pantry during periodic food donation drives.
3. Help pack food during the weekend—many volunteers ranging in age from seven to seventy do this noble work on weekends.
4. Donate money to a local food pantry.
5. Work in a homeless shelter preparing breakfast, lunch, and dinner.
6. Serve on the board of a food depository.

There are several national organizations that help the hungry in the United States, and virtually every community has a food pantry to help the hungry. The people in need vary, with bad economic times stretching the capacity of the food banks and pantries. The Greater Chicago Food Depository (GCFD) serves more than eight hundred thousand hungry people in Chicago through 650 food pantries located all over the city. Nutritious food, along with fresh produce, is provided to the pantries, which then help the community in their neighborhood. In addition to providing food, it is helping the poor develop careers in the catering and restaurant industry by teaching them to run a community kitchen. The food cooked by the trainees in the kitchen is served at several after-school programs in Chicago.

Global Food Banking Network (GFN) in Chicago is helping many countries set up food banks to serve the hungry in their countries. Working with leaders in various countries, and donors in the United States and around the world, GFN is helping fight hunger in thirty countries. Food Banks recover food that is being wasted (including fresh produce) and distribute it efficiently to people in need. Government food programs utilize food banks for distributing the food to the people in need. This is a great service that food banks provide, since their efficiency eliminates the food waste that is encountered in many government programs.

Food banks also assist with food programs in schools. The GCFD packs nutritious food for children from poor communities for weekends and for summer. The food packed by food banks and distributed to food pantries ensures that nutrition requirements for the poor are met. Getting personally involved in a food bank will make you feel good that you are helping your neighbors in the community.

Coauthor Dr. Raj Rajaram working in the Greater Chicago Food Depository in March, 2017

Rajaram's Story

In 1994, I attended a luncheon organized by the GCFD for lawyers and the legal profession. I was impressed by the way they were collecting all the food that was donated by companies and individuals and distributing it effectively throughout Cook County, Illinois. I visited their facility in the fall of 1994 and saw for myself the passionate people working in GCFD to help the hungry. I decided to donate regularly to GCFD, since alleviating hunger is a high priority for me. I went on a few weekends every year to help pack the large quantities of food donated to GCFD into packages required by the food pantries.

Since 1994, I have followed all the different programs initiated by GCFD to help the hungry in Cook County. I take visitors from India to GCFD so that they can replicate it in India. I was gratified that in 2012, through the connections in India of my friend in Oak Brook, Illinois, and the active assistance of GFN, Indian Food Banking Network (IFBN) was started in New Delhi, India. My friends in New Delhi helped me to get the food distribution started. A Chicago company, Griffith Laboratories, took the lead and started a food depository in Bengaluru, India, in 2014. Other cities in India are now getting their food banks started.

American leadership is helping India and many other countries set up their food banking network. This is improving the food distribution network for communities around the world. Philanthropic donations and countless volunteer hours feed millions of people through food pantries and food banks around the world.

Legal Services

Justice delayed is justice denied. Many poor people around the United States do not know how to access the legal system or are unable to find lawyers they can afford. Legal Assistance Foundations help the needy, and many bar associations are always looking for lawyers to help the poor pro bono. In addition, they need other professionals to help with the business aspects of the law practice. Volunteering with legal assistance foundations is very rewarding, and you can help a lot of people in dire straits get back on their feet.

Legal assistance can include many areas, but the areas one might consider for helping others include

1. divorce and other family matters;
2. rental eviction or other rental property issues;
3. applying for government assistance programs;
4. immigration issues;
5. domestic violence; and
6. business startups and other business issues.

Our government provides free public defenders for poor criminal defendants, but in civil cases, the funding support for legal assistance foundations is very minimal; they rely on volunteers and attorneys who have a passion to help the poor. In addition, monetary donations by individuals and law firms allow these foundations to provide their services to the poor.

Music and Arts Organizations

Do you like music? If you play an instrument or sing, you probably know groups where you would fit in. Perhaps a barbershop quartet, a local choir, or a town band? As an amateur, you may fit in, and even if you don't think you have the right stuff, there is no harm in trying. But say you don't have those talents—then what should you do? As many, even most, musical groups are short on funds, they rely on volunteers from the local scene, from music boosters for the schools to a symphony orchestra or anything in between. You probably know of some or can find notices in the local paper or on posters in store windows. You could be the one placing the posters, gaining friends at local businesses in the process. There are many other things you could do—publicity, ticket sales, board memberships, ushering at concerts, and more! In the Chicago area, there's a great group called the Saints whose members usher at ticketed events, big and small. As volunteers, they aren't paid, but they get to pick concerts they'd like to attend. It's a win-win—free ushering for the group and free attendance for the individual. Regardless of your availability and willingness, you are in demand—suit your interest to the needs you see.

Homelessness

Homelessness is caused by various reasons, the primary ones being mental illness or estrangement from family. The vagaries and ups and downs of the economic cycle drive some people to homelessness, but there are many government and voluntary services to help the homeless. One organization doing good work to help the homeless in DuPage County, Illinois, is PADS (Public Action to Deliver Shelter). This organization provides temporary housing for the homeless in homes that are owned by PADS and in shelters across the county. They work with churches and volunteers to provide shelter and meals over the weekends.

Even in affluent counties, some people will always be homeless and hungry. Keith Olson and his wife joined many other volunteers for years at a PADS site. Once a week, a local church opened its community room to those who had no home. The facility was functional and nothing more, literally a pad on the floor, but for those in need, it provided a place to sleep out of the weather and gave them supper, breakfast, and a bag lunch. If you have ambition to write the great American novel, this is the place for source material. You can hear hard luck stories you couldn't imagine and, surprise, some of the folks come from backgrounds just like yours. Another church, with contributions from others in the area, runs a food pantry. Most of the effort is voluntary, including acquiring and sorting the food and staffing the distribution location. A volunteer from the food pantry staffs a table at a farmers' market, taking donations of food bought at the market as well as the all-important cash. You likely have similar efforts in your area, and the volunteer could be you. Even if you don't have an ongoing program, there's probably a need, and you could start a similar effort, by yourself or with friends, or even better, by enlisting a church or service organization.

Another organization is Bridge Communities. It was started by a few businessmen in 1988, and it is now helping with free housing, education and skills training, and various other efforts to make the homeless economically independent within a two-year time frame. Volunteer opportunities for serving the homeless include

- tutoring children and adults;
- providing assistance with resume writing, interviewing, and getting a job;
- providing weekly mentoring to help families get back on their feet;
- job skills training and assistance in finding a job; and
- helping on weekends at churches that serve the homeless.

Are there people in need in your community? You can give of your time and money right in your town. Meals on Wheels also uses volunteers, delivering food to folks who can't get out, but interestingly, sometimes the deliverers are older than the recipients. For Meals on Wheels, ask around or check www.mowaa.org. If you are not sure if those are available or are looking for something else, your town or county probably has some sort of social services office that can give you leads on whatever you are interested in.

Job Training and Entrepreneur Development

Retired people have many skills and experiences and can share them with the next generation. The Executive Service Corps is a great organization that helps young entrepreneurs prepare business plans and get financing for their ideas. If you want to open a business in Chicago, go to http://esc-chicago.org/ in order to obtain excellent assistance from professionals who can help you prepare the documents needed to launch a successful business. The pitfalls and regulatory requirements for starting and succeeding in a business can be identified by ESC volunteers, and you can avoid many mistakes. Mentoring young entrepreneurs is very satisfying.

All labor unions and many community organizations have job-training programs, and you can volunteer your expertise and years of experience to help the people in the program. Volunteering at community colleges is another way of helping your community and having a fulfilling role in your retirement. Working with young people keeps you young, and seeing their progress in their career is very fulfilling.

Other Ways of Giving

Many people serve their community in unique ways suited to their skills and time availability. If you are a carpenter, you could form a group of carpenters and build furniture to give to poor schools in the United States. You could help Habitat for Humanity build homes for the poor. If you are a blacksmith or electrician, you can work in a community college or local museum rebuilding things or teaching others the trade. You can volunteer with the local emergency response teams (they will provide the needed training) or become a voluntary fire fighter. So, irrespective of your skill or financial capacity to give, you can help others in your community.

CHAPTER 4

Opportunities and Challenges Internationally

Bottom-Up Approach to International Community Development

Many international development agencies offer funds to the governments of developing countries by engaging with government officials, and the funds and expertise trickle down from the top, little of it reaching the beneficiaries. By being a volunteer for organizations like the Engineers Without Borders-International (EWB-International) and Médicins Sans Frontières (Doctors Without Borders), you can reverse this trend by affecting change from the bottom up. The United Nations Sustainable Development Goals (United Nations, 2016) delineates seventeen goals which should be implemented to improve the conditions of the poor in continents around the world:

1. No poverty
2. Zero hunger
3. Good health and well being
4. Quality education
5. Gender equality

6. Clean water and sanitation
7. Affordable and clean energy
8. Decent work and economic growth
9. Industry, innovation, and infrastructure
10. Reduced inequalities
11. Sustainable cities and communities
12. Responsible consumption and production
13. Climate action
14. Life below water
15. Life on land
16. Peace, justice, and strong institutions
17. Partnership for the goals

As we see from the above list, anyone who wants to help his or her fellow human beings around the world has plenty of opportunity. The last goal is particularly important, since the partnership that is happening among countries and institutions is very significant. École Polytechnique Fédéral de Lausanne in Lausanne, Switzerland, trains many people from around the world in Cooperation and Development (CODEV). The projects, many funded by United Nations Educational, Scientific, and Cultural Organization (UNESCO), are geared to help the developing world achieve these development goals. Many of these goals are yet to be achieved in the United States, and you can take up one of these goals with an organization that is working in your neighborhood.

Let us analyze these goals and how your involvement can make an impact. Detailed descriptions of opportunities available for giving in the international arena are provided later in the chapter. We will briefly describe what you can do to make a difference in these goals. The first goal is overly broad and encompasses a decent wage for work done and providing opportunities for citizens living in the inner cities and rural areas where poverty is prevalent. Getting involved in citizen advocacy is important to achieve this goal. The work by Porus Dadabhoy with the Citizen Advocacy Center in Illinois provides an example of the impact you can make by getting involved in changing local, state and federal policies impacting poverty (see chapter 8, Inspirational Stories).

Zero hunger is a lofty goal, and it can be achieved if the food distribution system is made truly efficient. We grow enough food and have good storage facilities, but distribution in the community is inefficient. My involvement with food banking in India and Chicago has convinced me that if a dedicated group of local citizens organizes a food bank in the community, the food distribution bottlenecks can be solved and food pantries can deliver the food to the needy on a regular basis. Besides clean water, there is no more basic need than food. Governments have come up with various ways to feed the hungry, but these programs are not as efficient as local food banks that deliver the food efficiently to the needy in the community. In Cook County, Illinois, the Greater Chicago Food Depository feeds eight hundred thousand hungry people every year through more than six hundred food pantries located all over the county. Good health and well-being is an area in which major strides have been made by eliminating many diseases in the developing world through vaccination programs. Organizations like Rotary International and Lions Clubs International have teamed up with philanthropists to eliminate disease and improve the health of the poor in Africa, Asia, and Latin/South America. By joining the local chapters of these organizations, you can make an impact on the good health and well-being of people around the world. Many US organizations organize ten-day trips to areas of the world needing help, and joining one of these is just one more way you can make a difference in the lives of the poor around the world.

Quality education is necessary to improve the economic well-being of the poor in many parts of the world. Access to schools is limited in many parts of Africa and Latin/South America, and even if schools are accessible, as in India, the quality of the education is poor because of the lack of trained teachers and educational materials. This is being addressed by several non-governmental organizations to supplement the education provided by government schools. Efforts in the United States and other places to reduce the digital divide by providing low-cost computers and online education is a major step in providing quality education. Reducing child labor through international cooperation is another way to provide quality education to the children in the developing world.

Gender equality is a goal that requires a change of mind-set in many parts of the world. There are deep-rooted beliefs about the roles of men and women in society, and unless these are changed dramatically in many parts of the world, gender equality will be hard to achieve. However, in the less than one hundred years since women got the right to vote in the United States, gender equality has come a long way. Women are represented in all professions that formerly were only occupied by men. Still, income equality among genders has not been fully achieved, even though there are laws that require this. Islamic countries have a long way to go in gender equality; there are places around the world where girls are still not allowed to attend school or boys are given preference over girls when it comes to access to schools.

Clean water and sanitation is an area where a lot of monetary resources are being spent by the UN and governments around the world. Technologies have been developed to reduce the cost of providing clean water to poor people and to improve access to sanitation. Despite all these efforts, more than a billion people lack access to clean water and sanitation. Many non-profit organizations are attempting to fill this gap, but it will take a lot more effort to provide this basic need to many people around the world. There are many opportunities to get involved in this effort, and one organization

I work with that is mobilizing students and engineers to do this work is Engineers Without Borders. Inspirational stories of people providing this service in rural areas of India are provided in this book.

The emergence of low-cost solar panels and different solar power technologies has made clean energy available to many communities around the world that have had no access to reliable power. The Paris Climate Change Accords provided millions of dollars for renewable energy in developing countries, and this is enabling many social entrepreneurs to work for renewable energy. Subsidies provided by governments for renewable energy are also providing clean energy to many with no access to the grid. Many volunteer opportunities are available for senior citizens to help with clean energy, either by raising funds or by getting involved in clean energy projects in their community and around the world.

The whole world is working on improving the lives of people by creating jobs through Industry and Infrastructure. Senior citizens with all kinds of life and professional experience can give back in a big way to their diaspora, since a majority of Americans came to this country from different parts of the world. I have been transferring US environmental technologies and management capabilities to India for many years, and many of my fellow Indian American friends have been doing their part to help with development projects in India for many years as well.

The United States is a leader in ending inequalities, and our constitution protects citizens irrespective of color, race, gender, national origin, and sexual orientation. We can spread this message to parts of the world that do not enjoy this protection, and we can volunteer to educate girls and change policies around the world that will ensure equality to all global citizens. Volunteers in communities in the United States and other parts of the world are helping restoring equality so that all citizens can be productive and happy.

Our cities are growing, and more rural populations are moving to cities. We have to make the cities and communities sustainable by improving governance, using technologies effectively to save water, energy, and natural resources, and converting our wastes to energy. Cities around the world are looking for expertise and volunteers who can plan, design and implement solutions for smart cities. Many opportunities exist for getting involved in sustainable cities and communities around the world.

Climate Action is a worldwide effort; two hundred countries signed an agreement to work together on controlling climate change and saving our planet in 2015 in Paris, France. Give your talent, time, and treasure to improve our planet; irrespective of your professional experience, you can contribute to minimize global warming. Something as simple as conserving energy and water improves our planet. But you can also teach your grandchildren and kids in your neighborhood about climate change and global warming. Work with organizations like the Audubon Society and World Wildlife Fund to minimize species extinction. Work with local community organizations that are working hard for a sustainable future and to leave a better world for our children.

Peace, justice, and strong institutions are critical for a peaceful world. Chapter 8, Inspirational Stories, is devoted to citizen advocacy, and details how one person got involved in this important task. If you have experience in building strong institutions, you can share this experience with communities in Africa, India, and other parts of the world. There are many organizations bringing people together to foster peace in troubled areas of the globe, and you can join one of them to help with world peace. If you have a legal background, you can work for justice in our inner cities as well as any part of the world. We are truly blessed to have many organizations that are working hard to establish peace and justice around the world, and volunteering for them is the easiest way to get involved.

Specific Opportunities for Getting Involved

The world is shrinking with the use of the Internet and social media. Any worthwhile cause around the world, if properly conveyed to donors, mobilizes support from a large group of donors from all corners of the world. When a large tsunami hit Asia in 2004, millions of dollars were raised once Google put the cause on its homepage. Various organizations can help you satisfy the passion you have to serve in any part of the world. Join a global movement to help others; this way you help yourself (Kristof and WuDunn, 2009). We have to help others to help ourselves become better. Connection to something larger and a great cause helps us with sustained happiness.

US citizens have roots (one generation or several generations apart) all over the world. Using these roots, we are doing good for people around the world while helping people in our community. The giving comes in various forms:

- traveling to anywhere in the world and providing your expertise to a nonprofit organization (Engineers Without Borders, Médicins Sans Frontières, and so on.)
- giving a donation to support work of a nongovernmental organization in a part of the world where you want to help
- traveling to any part of the world to help a US nonprofit organization like Rotary International or Lions Clubs International or a local nonprofit for recovering from a disaster such as an earthquake or flood
- giving your time and talent on a regular basis within the United States to assist a nonprofit working around the world

During the past forty-five years, the number of people living outside their country of origin has increased from 76 million to 215 million (www.usaid.gov). In 2012, the amount of remittances to friends and families in the developing world from these people was $534 billion. The International

Diaspora Engagement Alliance (www.diasporaalliance.org) was formed by the US Department of State and helps people from the diaspora living in the United States to give back to their countries of origin. The main pillars of this alliance are *entrepreneurship, innovation, philanthropy and volunteerism*.

Diaspora from Africa, the Caribbean, and Latin America are active through the marketplace initiatives that the US Agency for International Development (USAID) conducts periodically. In addition, IDEA regularly conducts annual workshops and programs for citizen immigrants to engage with their country of origin.

Organizations in the United States that work around the world are plentiful, with Rotary International and Lions Clubs International being the largest, present in more than two hundred countries. Once you narrow down your area of interest, the country where you would like to make a difference, the opportunities available become clear. Subsequently, you can research the organizations that are doing work in the country and in your area of interest. Talking to friends who have served in the country will help you figure out the dos and don'ts. Learning the culture by reading books about the country and meeting people from the diaspora will help a lot in planning your philanthropic trip. Just like you plan your regular vacation, you can plan your philanthropic vacation where you are involved in giving back to the community you visit in another country. Many countries in Africa have tour packages geared to philanthropic giving.

Churches and service organizations arrange medical and humanitarian missions around the world. They do all the preliminary work and select the nongovernmental or beneficiary organization, arrange all the logistics, and make it easy for donors to give their time and money to make a difference in the lives of people served by the beneficiary organization. My brother went to Honduras on a mission with the Rotary Club in Milwaukee and came back happy that he had touched so many children's lives and their families during the one-week trip. My Lions Club in Oak Brook made it possible for one of our members to go to Guatemala for a week of service through her church. We helped her and her husband with their expenses, and they came back energized after a week of service.

Areas of Involvement

Intervention by volunteers is needed around the world in the following categories:

- Health
- Hunger
- Education
- Energy
- Livelihoods
- Environment/Water
- Human Trafficking
- Refugees
- Women, Children, and Social Justice

Health

Health issues vary from facial deformities to fighting infectious disease in various parts of the world. My friend in Canada goes around the world to help with surgeries for cleft palate. He says that the two weeks he spends every year providing anesthesia for these surgeries are the best part of his life. I really admire the volunteers who go to fight infectious disease wherever it happens around the world. The Ebola crisis in Africa was brought under control with the help of professionals from the United States along with nurse volunteers. These volunteers risked their lives to help people in Liberia and neighboring countries. Experienced seniors are taking such opportunities and enriching their lives while helping poor people stay healthy and avoid easily treatable diseases in parts of the Caribbean, Latin America, South America, Asia, and Africa.

The life span of seniors has increased significantly in the last fifty years in the United States, with people living into their eighties and nineties in good health. How do we make this abundance of good health available to others around the world? Many physicians, healthcare professionals, and volunteers are traveling to many parts of the world to work with local nonprofits, which are trying their best with the limited resources they have available. Organizations like Partners for Health are focusing on long-term involvement in a country, and many seniors are helping with ongoing projects in Haiti.

There are many international volunteer programs for seniors that involve working in community centers, orphanages, and health-care centers where seniors help develop activities and assist in feeding, cleaning, and health care. Organizations such as Volunteers for Peace, the Peace Corps, International Volunteer HQ, Bamboo, and Volunteering Solutions all have health-care-related programs that accept senior volunteers. Trips range in cost, duration, and activities—there are plenty to choose from!

Here are a few examples of volunteer programs that relate to health care that seniors can engage in:

- **The Peace Corps** is always looking for health-care and education-program specialists all over the world. Locations range from Africa to Central America to Europe and involve mentoring, training, and assisting Peace Corps partners in equipping families and local community health workers with knowledge about healthy habits and behaviors. This could include supporting healthy births, addressing basic hygiene issues, and helping to decrease unnecessary death and disease (mainly focused on mothers and children).

- **Bamboo**, a Uganda-based volunteer program, looks to improve public health. Volunteers work alongside local grassroots initiatives in Uganda to ensure better health among individuals in communities and children in secondary schools. They also work to increase general health awareness in Ugandan communities. Roles also allow you to get involved in mentoring in rural communities with teens on issues such as drug abuse, sexual education, and general health care.
- **International Volunteer HQ** has opportunities worldwide in the areas of physiotherapy, pharmacy, dentistry, paramedics, clinical lab science, emergency medicine, speech therapy, optometry, nutrition, public health, orthopedics, radiology, HIV/AIDS support, midwifery, and pediatrics. This allows for retired healthcare professionals to truly use their skills in meaningful ways. The settings include clinics, hospitals, and assisted living homes in Africa, Central America, the South Pacific, and the UK.
- **Volunteering Journeys** includes destinations such as India, Thailand, South Africa, Cambodia, Bali, Sri Lanka, and Nepal. Medical and healthcare volunteers include those with experience in nursing, pediatrics, pathology, physical therapy, physiotherapy, radiotherapy, ultrasound, gynecology, ophthalmology, orthopedics, accident & emergency, anesthetics, biochemistry, dentistry, ENT, general surgery, maternity & midwifery, yoga therapy, occupational therapy, pharmacy, and naturopathy and alternative medicine such as Ayurveda.
- **Volunteering Solutions** has international destinations for medical volunteers including the Philippines, Thailand, Cambodia, Vietnam, Tanzania, South Africa, Ghana, Kenya, Peru, and Costa Rica. Projects span from one to six weeks, and participants joining these programs usually work under the supervision of professional doctors and nurses as well as support staff and assist them in the treatment of patients. These projects are most suited for retired medical professionals, as all interested candidates are required to provide a copy of their educational medical qualifications.

Public health systems in many countries around the world are weak, which means that disease prevention or preventing the spread of epidemics is weak. Many of these countries are in Africa and Latin America, and opportunities for Americans to help thousands of people exist. The recent experience of the Ebola epidemic showed the importance of American intervention by the government and volunteers. The Department of State and the Centers for Disease Control post many of these opportunities on their websites, and retired health-care professionals can make a huge impact by volunteering their time, talent, and treasure.

Prevention of disease is a challenge in many parts of the world, since access to clean water and adequate sanitation is minimal. There are many organizations in the United States working these issues in Asia, Africa, Latin America, and South America. Engineers Without Borders (www.ewb-usa.org) has professional chapters where retired or semiretired engineers can volunteer their time and experience to work on water and sanitation projects. They also mentor young engineers and engineering students to help student chapters complete their projects in many parts of the world. My personal experience in doing such projects with young engineers from the United States and India has been a highlight of my forty-year career in engineering.

Hunger
Hunger and malnutrition are the easiest preventable problems the world faces. This is the low hanging fruit that can be tackled through existing organizations and volunteers. Countries in sub-Saharan Africa go through cycles of severe drought, and it makes the headlines for a few days and then is forgotten. Organizations like the Global FoodBanking Network (GFN) and Second Harvest are working to alleviate hunger in developing countries and also within the United States. All other interventions mentioned in this chapter will not be effective until the problems of hunger and malnutrition are addressed. Many diseases can be prevented if malnutrition, especially of children, is solved.

VASUDEVAN RAJARAM, KEITH OLSON AND ANDREA GRONER

Statistics compiled by US food banks show that one in eight people go hungry at one time or other in their lifetime. This is an alarming statistic, since we are the food basket for the world yet we pay farmers *not* to produce food. It is a problem of distribution and making it available to those in need. Chicago's Food Bank has more than six hundred neighborhood outlets and feeds more than eight hundred thousand people in Cook County. When I (Rajaram) have volunteered at Chicago's Food Bank, I have seen volunteers of all ages repack the large food donations received into smaller sizes for distribution to the food pantries around Chicago. Volunteering with your time, talent (improve their processes), and treasure is welcome at all food banks.

GFN (Global FoodBanking Network), located in Chicago, helps many countries set up food banks and teaches them how to manage them effectively. I have helped GFN set up food banks in India, and they are serving a lot of the hungry people in the National Capital Region of Delhi and many other cities. Their annual meeting brings together food banking managers from thirty countries to interact and learn to expand their operations and run them effectively. Major food producers and distributors around the world support this effort and donate food in large quantities to food banks. If you have expertise in logistics or fundraising or international institutions, you should get involved in helping food banks propagate all over the world so that the local folks can control the distribution of the food and make it available to vulnerable populations.

The US Agency for International Development (USAID) has initiated several programs to alleviate hunger around the world. They are transferring technology on agriculture and helping small farmers increase their productivity. They contract with US universities and private companies to provide expertise and food distribution to countries that are facing hunger. USAID has relieved malnutrition and hunger in many parts of the world. If you want to assist USAID or their contractors in this effort, there are many opportunities. If your expertise is required by USAID, you can apply to be a consultant and help suffering in any part of the world that you like. Apart from travel and great experiences, you will be fulfilling a basic need.

Undernourishment around the World, 1990 to 2014				
Number of undernourished and prevalence (percentage of population) of undernourishment				
	1990 Number*	1990 Percentage	2014 Number*	2014 Percentage
World	1,010.6	18.6	794.6	10.9
Developed Regions	20.0	<5	14.7	<5
Developing Regions	990.7	23.3	779.9	12.9
Africa	181.7	27.6	232.5	20.0
Sub-Saharan Africa	175.7	33.2	220	23.2
Asia	741.9	23.6	511.7	12.1
Eastern Asia	295.4	23.2	145.1	9.6
Southeastern Asia	137.5	30.6	60.5	9.6
Southern Asia	291.2	23.9	281.4	15.7
Latin America/Caribbean	66.1	14.7	34.3	5.5
Oceania	1.0	15.7	1.4	14.2

*Numbers in millions. Source: FAO The State of Food Insecurity in the World 2015, p. 8.

Education

Teach for America has spawned Teach for India and other similar programs around the world. Young people are doing this under government or private grants, but seniors can do this to help poor children around the world. I (Rajaram) am involved with a school in India called Little Stars School, where volunteers from America and Europe stay for periods from one month to nine months to teach the children from poor neighborhoods. The impact these volunteers make is huge, but the great thing is that when you ask these volunteers about their experience, they say it does more for them than the benefit to the children. Humans feel good in helping others, and opportunities for doing this are available in many parts of the world. A young woman from South Bend, Indiana, has signed up to teach kids through a nonprofit in India called Yuwa (meaning youth in Hindi) India (www.yuwa-india.org). She gave up her secure job to go and teach the children in India for free for one year. How much more can be done by retired seniors in countries like India and Africa?

With technology, you don't have to travel long distances but can reach the students from any part of the world through Skype or Google hangouts. My friend in San Francisco teaches children in India to speak English through Skype. An organization called Pratham (www.pratham.org) organizes the teaching session, and my retired friend participates in the program regularly. My friend in Naperville, Illinois, reaches out to college students in India through Google hangouts. With YouTube and various other electronic media, such interactions are getting more frequent among senior volunteers in the United States and young people in other countries around the world. He teaches them the soft skills of time management, quality management, and other topics that they do not learn in college since it is not part of their curriculum.

The USA chapter of Pratham (www.prathamusa.org) mobilizes funds from the United States for helping the education of millions of poor children in

India. I have had the privilege of leading the Chicago chapter of PrathamUSA for five years, and it is heart-warming to see that the funds I collect from donors in Chicago is helping the education of more than ten thousand underprivileged children per year in India. It takes persistence and persuasion to collect these funds through many fund-raising events, but when I see the smiling faces of children that the funds help educate, it is very gratifying. Mobilizing donors of all ages for the cause has been a great learning experience, and it keeps me motivated to work hard to grow the chapter in Chicago. In 2010, when I was given the opportunity to head the chapter of PrathamUSA in Chicago, I felt unsure if I could raise funds for this cause, which I completely believed in. However, once I talked to people I knew and convinced them of the cause, they donated generously of their time, talent, and treasure.

Anyone can do the same as I have done; it just takes hard, consistent work to raise funds for the cause you believe in. Once you break out of your comfort zone, however, amazing things are possible, and you may surprise yourself. Corporate America is eager to help good causes, so it's important to know how to approach them for the benefit of your cause. Individuals are keen to help a good cause as well, but persistence is needed to raise the money. Above all, the pleasure you get from helping others gives purpose to life.

North South Foundation (www.northsouth.org) helps children in the United States reach academic excellence through spelling and math bees and also collects money for providing scholarships to deserving students all over India. The recipients of the scholarship have done well in college, and as they became successful, began to give back through their own programs to improve education in rural areas. It shows the impact that one organization in Chicago can have on improving the education and lives of thousands of children at home and in India. If all seniors got involved in some way in giving back to the improvement of education in our local area or internationally, the world would be a much better place, with less violence and more economic prosperity.

Thanks to international governmental and philanthropic efforts, the number of children out of school has drastically dropped in the last few decades. Graphics courtesy of the World Bank Group, 2016 World Development Indicators.

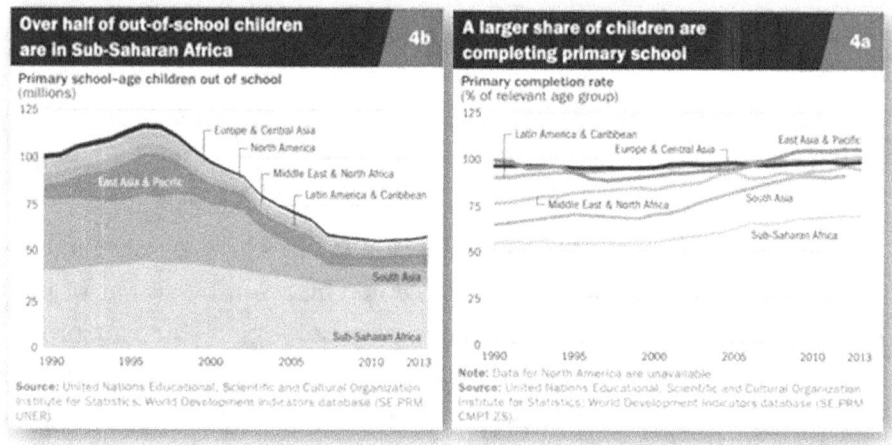

Energy

Many parts of India, Africa, and Latin America are not connected to an electric grid and must conduct all their activities during daylight hours only. The children in these communities suffer since they cannot study after the sun goes down. With the availability of solar lighting, these off-grid communities are thriving, since the people are able to make a better living and children do well in school. My (Dr. Rajaram's) friend in Chicago wanted to provide solar lights to several villages in India. He had a small fund-raising event with his friends and relatives. He raised about $8,000 from this effort, and with that, he applied to Rotary

International Foundation in Evanston, Illinois, for their support. They gave him a two to one match, which gave him $24,000 for his project. He then connected with an organization in India (The Energy Research Institute) that was willing to give him a three to one match. So finally he had $96,000 to launch his solar lighting project.

Working with a well-established non-governmental organization in India (Deendayal Research Institute) as the local partner, he was able to establish solar lights for forty rural villages in India. He found several local entrepreneurs who would use the funds to buy a large solar charging station for each village and several solar lamps for giving to the villagers. The entrepreneur takes a nominal fee to cover his costs and profit and charges the lamp batteries every week. The value of teamwork and getting the right people to support your effort is exhibited by this story. The lives of the residents of these forty villages have improved tremendously due to the dedicated efforts of one senior in Chicago who had an idea and implemented it. The children in these villages can study well and become valuable citizens of India.

Solar installations for schools and computer laboratories are required in many parts of the world. Local nonprofits are undertaking these efforts, and with a small donation of money, time, and talent, seniors can improve the quality of education in these schools by helping with solar energy installations. If you have the talent, you can join an Engineers Without Borders team in the area where you live (visit www.ewb-usa.org) and help with the improvement of schools. Small-scale hydroelectric plants are also sources of energy in many rural areas of the world. I know of student chapters in the United States looking for mentors for such projects, which they are undertaking as part of their college experience. Such opportunities keep seniors connected to students while helping the poor in many parts of the world.

Livelihoods

There is a saying that is widely used in development: "Teach a person to fish instead of just giving food." To put this saying into practice, we need to assist communities around the world in providing opportunities for livelihoods. Based on the strengths of the community and the natural resources available in the area, livelihood projects can be designed. In addition to supporting these projects, we need to help develop markets for the products made by the community. FXB Suraksha, based in Delhi, has developed a successful model of supporting a community for three years to make them economically independent. They impart livelihood skills and help the community market the products they make to markets in India and the United States. For example, in West Bengal, where there is an abundance of jute available, they teach the community to make various colorful household and commercial products using jute and then help them sell the products to make a decent living.

A job gives self-confidence, economic independence, and a sense of pride. The concept of microloans was popularized by Mohammed Younus of Bangladesh in the late 1990s. The UN is now promoting microloans in Africa, Asia, and other parts of the world. US organizations like Opportunity International, Kiva, and Heifer International are providing opportunities to individuals to donate small amounts of money to enable them to provide microloans to individuals in developing countries to start their own businesses. In addition to providing funds for these microloans, a senior can provide his or her talent and time to volunteer for livelihood projects run by such reputable organizations.

Many livelihood projects in India are organized and managed by nongovernmental organizations (NGOs). These NGOs have well-established networks in many communities and are involved in skills training and job creation. They run vocational training programs that help the poor earn their livelihood and support their families. The range of the livelihood projects involves making good quality paper from paper waste to making handicrafts and home goods using local materials. These NGOs are also looking for help in selling their products in the United States, and you can help them provide outlets through your connections. One young man who was provided vocational training by Pratham in the hospitality business has helped his rural family while earning a respectable living in a city.

Environment/Water

The lack of clean water impacts over a billion people around the world. The Gates Foundation and other organizations like Rotary International and Water.org are mobilizing funds for making clean water accessible to all. A company in Beaverton, Oregon, Puralytics, has come up with a solar technology to clean dirty water ponds and a solar bag to purify water in a few hours with exposure to the sun. The US Agency for International Development (USAID) is spending millions of dollars every year to provide clean water to many parts of the world, including war-torn Palestine. The United Nations Development Program (and other groups within the UN) is the leading organization that is funding clean water programs around the world.

If you have a passion to help provide clean water to poor communities around the world, you can mobilize funds and partner with organizations mentioned above and many others to realize your passion. Many philanthropists are working to solve the problem of clean drinking water for the poor around the world. You can connect those in need with these philanthropists and watch magical things happen. Researching the people in need and connecting them with people who want to help them is a great use of your time and talent for research. You can also connect communities with the government resources available and help them write grant applications to secure the funds. So there are many ways of helping poor people who do not have clean water or who live in a dirty environment.

Rajaram's Story

My story in this regard is what anyone can do in their own small way to help provide clean water. My friend in St. Paul, Minnesota, called me in 2003 and said that he would like $200 from me to provide clean water for a community of eleven hundred in South India. I asked him how he could do it with my $200. He said, "I have designed a water reservoir in a drought-stricken part of south India, and if they have to utilize the rains that they get for about a month a year, they need this twenty-foot deep water reservoir. The cost of the reservoir is $6,000 (I was surprised at the low cost), since the villagers are going to give their sweat equity for the project. In addition, I asked them to mobilize $2,000 from their community, and they did. The local government matched it, and for the $2,000 remaining, I am asking ten friends to donate $200 each." This really opened my eyes to the possibility of helping others for a mere $200, since many others were involved in this effort. I have been tracking that community since then, and the amazing improvement in the whole community, including the children, is really gratifying.

My friend in Downers Grove, Illinois, read a story about a community in India that was termed by Green Peace as the "worst polluted area of the world." Industry had grown rampantly over the years without implementing the required environmental measures to clean the water and air. He called me and a couple of others who are experts in treating impure water, and we decided to help. He arranged a visit for the two experts from Chicago to the industrial park where there were many polluting industries. He and the two experts visited the pollution control facilities and wrote an eleven-page report on the inadequacy of the treatment facilities and the major environmental harm the improperly treated discharges are doing to a river downstream, which is the main source of drinking water for many poor communities.

When there was no response from the treatment plant, they gave their report to the local press. Soon after, the government appointed a high-powered committee to analyze the situation and implement remedial measures. The committee, made up of experts, government officials, and industry representatives, recommended that new management take over the facility and demand accountability. Hence, an activist from Downers Grove, Illinois, could improve the environment ten thousand miles away by using his connections and by persisting in his desire to make a difference in water quality for thousands of poor people being impacted by the toxic discharges to the water bodies on which they rely for their water needs.

Huge strides have been made in the area of water access, but there is still a lot of work to be done, primarily in Sub-Saharan Africa. Graphics courtesy of the World Bank Group, 2016 World Development Indicators.

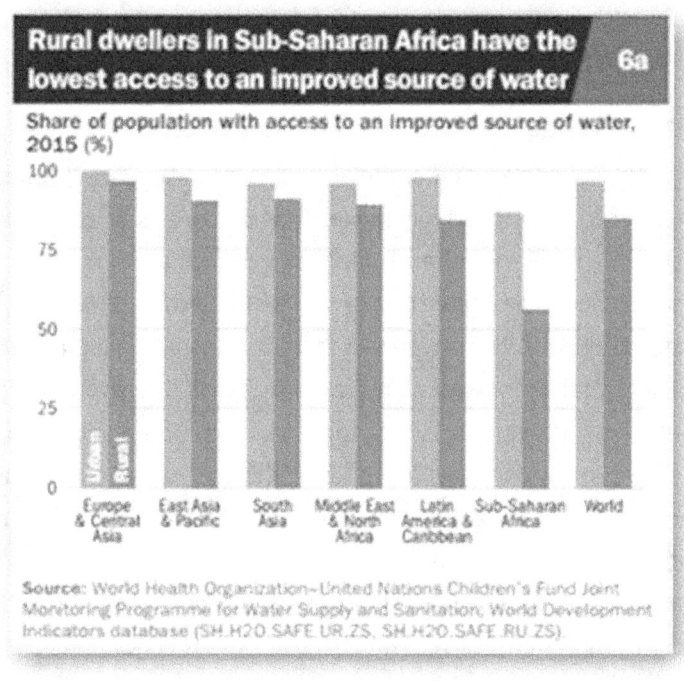

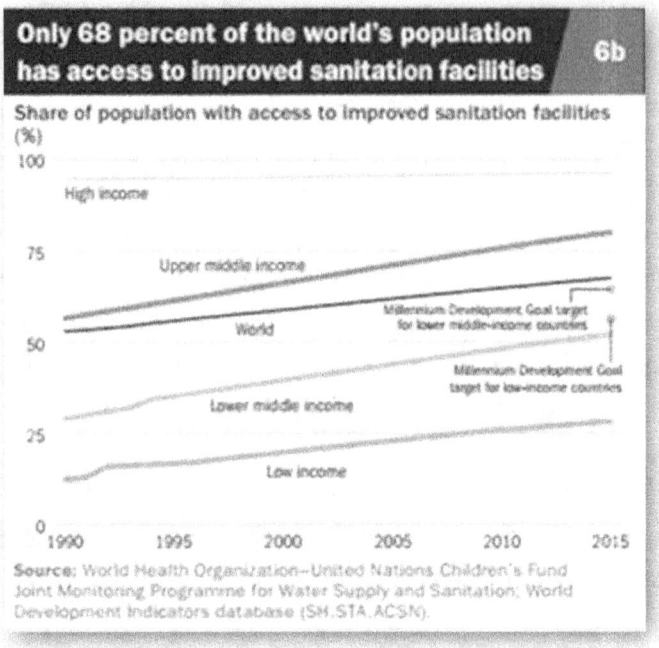

Human Trafficking

Human trafficking is the worst crime against humanity, since it forces an individual into forced labor or sexual slavery. It is defined as "modern day slavery and involves the use of force, fraud, or coercion to obtain some type of labor or commercial sex act." The United Nations Office on Drugs and Crimes (UNODC) is the guardian of the UN Convention against Transnational Organized Crime (UNTOC.) Their job is to assist states in their efforts to prevent, suppress, and punish trafficking in persons. Every year, thousands of men, women, and children fall in to the hands of traffickers, even though governments have passed laws against trafficking and the United Nations considers it a violation of human rights. It is the greed of individuals and organizations combined with the desperate poverty existing in many parts of the world that keeps this worst violation of human rights alive. The US government is doing its best to bring such crimes to light and sending those responsible to lengthy prison sentences, but enforcement is lax in many countries around the world.

There are several national and international nongovernmental organizations (NGOs) fighting to minimize human trafficking, and you can volunteer for them to make a difference:

- Polaris Project
- Purchased
- Anti-Slavery International
- Not for Sale
- Shared Hope International
- Global Alliance Against Trafficking
- Free the Slaves
- International Justice Mission
- ECPAT (End Child Prostitution in Asian Tourism)
- Prajwala (based in India)
- COSA (Children's Organization of Southeast Asia)
- Urban Light (specializing in male victims of trafficking)

Refugees

The refugee crisis happens with every war or major political upheaval around the world. It has become pronounced since after World War II, when many Europeans affected by the Holocaust and war decided to move out of Europe. Another major migration of refugees happened when the Indian subcontinent was divided into India and Pakistan after the British left their colony. A refugee is a person who is fleeing their country (by force or by choice) in order to escape war, persecution or natural disaster.

The UN Convention on Refugees was approved in July 1951 and became effective in April 1954. It was signed by 145 countries, and 146 countries, including the United States, approved the protocol for the convention in 1967. The UN High Commission for Refugees has been very busy during the influx of Syrian refugees into Turkey and Europe during the recent Syrian

Civil War. Millions of refugees have been pouring in from the war, and many volunteers in Europe have stepped up to help them. The International Refugee Committee (www.rescue.org) is a major nonprofit organization in the United States that helps refugees settle here. Volunteering for them or donating to them is one way you can do something to help a refugee who is accepted in the United States.

Church groups and other faith organizations do a lot for refugees in the process of settling down in a new city and finding employment. Government assistance to these organizations is very limited, and they rely on contributions from donors and volunteers to serve the needs of the refugees. Church World Service (www.cwsglobal.org) is a national charity that has been serving the needs of refugees for seventy years. It provides a welcoming community of volunteers and staff that find legal status for the refugees; resettle and rebuild their lives by helping them find shelter, food, and work; and mobilize local communities to help refugees learn English and adjust to life in the United States.

The United States has been accepting refugees for many years from many war-torn parts of the world. The recent influx of Syrian refugees caused by the Civil War in Syria has been managed by governments and volunteers in many countries of Europe, Canada, and the United States. Syrian Americans have been helping in this effort, just like Americans who hail from different parts of the world help refugees from their part of the world settle down in the United States. It is a very difficult process for the refugee to adjust to living in a US community, and local volunteers make this transition easier. Many opportunities are available in your community to help in refugee resettlement.

Amnesty International and the UN Refugee agency, Office for the Coordination of Humanitarian Affairs, and the International Organization of Migration provide these key facts about refugees:

- Gulf countries, including Qatar, United Arab Emirates, Saudi Arabia, Kuwait, and Bahrain, have offered zero resettlement places to Syrian refugees.
- Other high-income countries, including Russia, Singapore, and South Korea, have also offered zero resettlement places.

Germany has pledged 43,431 places for Syrian refugees via resettlement and other admission pathways; this is approximately 46 percent of the combined EU total.

- Excluding Germany, the remaining twenty-seven EU countries have pledged around 51,205 places via resettlement and other admission pathways, or around 1 percent of the Syrian refugee population in the main host countries.
- Germany and Sweden together received 64 percent of Syrian asylum applications in Europe between April 2011 and October 2016.
- 93 percent of Syrian refugees in urban areas in Jordan are living below the poverty line, as well as 70 percent of Syrian refugees in Lebanon, 65 percent in Egypt, and 37 percent in Iraq.

CHAPTER 5

Nonprofit Organizations

The godfathers of modern philanthropic studies, Robert Payton and Michael Moody, determined that there are seven main functions to philanthropy:

1. Reduce human suffering
2. Enhance human potential
3. Promote equity and justice
4. Build community
5. Provide human fulfillment
6. Support experimentation and change
7. Foster pluralism

Sometimes philanthropic action is used exclusively to accomplish one of these functions, but more often it accomplishes several of these purposes at once. These functions can be accomplished through informal philanthropic acts, such as person-to-person acts of kindness, but are by and large accomplished with formalized philanthropy through nonprofit organizations.

This chapter represents an overview of America's thriving nonprofit sector, which is vast and complex. This sector has grown dramatically, especially within the last few decades, and is comprised of 1.5 million nonprofits registered with the US Internal Revenue Service (IRS). It received more than $1.7 trillion in revenue and continuously accounts for between 5 and 10 percent of America's gross domestic product. The nonprofit sector touches every American household in one way or another, yet it is still widely underexplored and undertaught.

What Does It Mean to Have a Nonprofit "Sector"?

Generally, there are four main sectors into which American society is split. This attempts to account for all of the established organizations and their societal roles, as well as for family and relationships. These sectors are public and private, for-profit and nonprofit, and include everything else in between. While these four sectors are generally considered the formal division of societal functions, this division does not account for a plethora of things. For example, there are complex relationships between sectors, and oftentimes the sectors blur with one another. There are plenty of public/private partnerships that work together to solve societal issues, as well as social entrepreneurs (who operate for-profit businesses but also accomplish a social purpose).

Here are the four sectors:

- Government/public
- Business/private
- Nonprofit/third sector
- Informal sector (this includes things that are more intimate, like family and relationships)

The nonprofit sector is more visible than ever, and it has only been considered its own section of society since 1973. Before the Tax Reform Act of 1969, there were several questions that went unanswered about philanthropy's place in society. More than seven hundred individuals and organizations (under the leadership of John Rockefeller III and Aetna Insurance chairman John Filer) convened over a two-year period to participate in eighty-five separate studies focused on the third sector. In 1975, a 240-page report complete with data and suggestions was published. The report is popularly known as the Filer Commission. The commission defended the rights of Americans to distribute their wealth to nonprofits and foundations as a solution to public issues, as well as protected the rights of individuals to deduct charitable gifts from their taxes.

While this sector is only now being more broadly defined and studied, nonprofits and philanthropic action have played a huge role in American history. Abolitionists used associations and antislavery societies to carry out their work in the eighteen hundreds and played a huge part in the abolitionist movement leading up to the Civil War. Similarly, suffrage associations played a huge role in earning women the right to vote, and many organizations assisted protestors and change-makers in the civil rights movements of the 1960s. The nonprofit sector and Americans' need to associate with others with like causes have resulted in hundreds of years of historical change toward a more civil, civic-minded, and peaceful society.

Types of Nonprofit Organizations

While there are thirty different kinds of tax-exempt organizations that are considered nonprofits, generally when we refer to a nonprofit (with a charitable purpose), we are talking about a 501(c)(3) organization. These are organizations that fulfill a general "public good" or serve a mission that benefits society. *Giving USA*, a publication from the IU Lilly Family School of Philanthropy that serves as the epitome of research on this subject, has divided charitable giving into several categories:

- Religious
- Education

- Health
- Human Services
- Public (societal benefit)
- Arts, Culture, and Humanities
- Environmental and Animal
- International/Foreign Affairs
- Foundations
- Other

Most likely, the nonprofit organizations that you are familiar with are 501(c)(3)s. These are designated organizations that are eligible to give donors a tax write-off for their donation. We will go into more depth about what it takes to be a 501(c)(3) later in the chapter, but there are several types of organizations just within this category that accomplish their mission with different functionality, tactics, and operations.

Below is a list that outlines most important IRS Nonprofit Tax Codes:

501(c)(1) — Corporations Organized Under Act of Congress (including Federal Credit Unions)

501(c)(2) — Title Holding Corporation for Exempt Organization

501(c)(3) — Religious, Educational, Charitable, Scientific, Literary, Testing for Public Safety, to Foster National or International Amateur Sports Competition, or Prevention of Cruelty to Children or Animals Organizations

501(c)(4) — Civic Leagues, Social Welfare Organizations, and Local Associations of Employees

501(c)(5) — Labor, Agricultural, and Horticultural Organizations

501(c)(6) — Business Leagues, Chambers of Commerce, Real Estate Boards, and so on.

501(c)(7) — Social and Recreational Clubs

501(c)(8) — Fraternal Beneficiary Societies and Associations...
501(c)(21) — Black lung Benefit Trusts
501(c)(22) — Withdrawal Liability Payment Fund
501(c)(23) — Veterans Organization (created before 1880)
501(c)(25) — Title Holding Corporations or Trusts with Multiple Parents
501(c)(26) — State-Sponsored Organization Providing Health Coverage for High-Risk Individuals
501(c)(27) — State-Sponsored Workers' Compensation Reinsurance Organization
501(c)(28) — National Railroad Retirement Investment Trust

Public-Serving Organizations, The Nonprofit Bread and Butter

A nonprofit organization is loosely defined as any group that is not a family, not a business, and not part of government. There is no perfect definition for these kinds of organizations, except that they serve a public benefit as defined under the 501(c)(3) tax code. Appendix B provides details on how one can apply to obtain a 501(c)(3) status from the IRS. It details important record keeping and annual reporting requirements.

There are six main characteristics to 501(c)(3) nonprofits:

- Institutionalized
- Private, not part of government
- Not profit-distributing (there are no shareholders who receive profits, but rather the "profit" goes back into its programs)
- Self-governing
- Voluntary, noncompulsory, involving a meaningful degree of voluntary participation
- Serves a public good or benefit

Robert Payton defines philanthropy as "Voluntary action for the public good." This begs the question, however…What is the "public good"? This is such a broad and subjective concept that people in business, government, and philanthropy debate about what is public/societal benefit. That is the wonderful thing about philanthropic action—*you* decide what you think is the public good and then act accordingly.

The IRS defines 501(c)(3) nonprofits as:

> Corporations, and any community chest, fund, or foundation, organized and operated exclusively for religious, charitable, scientific testing for public safety, literary, or educational purposes, or to foster national or international amateur sports competition (but only if no part of its activities involves the provision of athletic facilities or equipment), or for the prevention of cruelty to children or animals, no part of the net earnings of which insures to the benefit of any private shareholder or individual, no substantial part of which is carrying on propaganda, or otherwise attempting to influence legislation, and which does not participate in, or intervene in (including the publishing or distribution of statements), any political campaign on behalf of (or in opposition to) any candidate for public office [Internal Revenue Code, sec. 501(c)(3)].

As of 2016, there were **1,571,056** tax-exempt organizations, including:

- 1,097,689 public charities
- 105,030 private foundations
- 368,337 other types of nonprofit organizations, including chambers of commerce, fraternal organizations, and civic leagues

(Source: NCCS Business Master File 4/2016)

Nonprofit MYTH BUSTER—"Nonprofits can get away with more."
While there may be the occasional news story sensationalizing a nonprofit manager's abuse of an organization's power or wealth, on the whole, the nonprofit sector is transparent and accountable for all of their actions. Nonprofits are required to publish their tax returns and CEO salaries and are asked regularly to provide lists of their funding sources, with the paperwork to back it up. This is very distinct to the nonprofit sector, and one would be hard-pressed to find this same information about a large for-profit business. You can find this information about any nonprofit on the organization's website or on charitable watchdog organizations like Charity Navigator and Guidestar.

Community Chests

A truly American branch of nonprofits is the "community chest." The United Way is the most notable of this kind of organization, as it is a money tank that vets organizations by impact and effectiveness, grants money, and generally supports the communities where they reside through philanthropy (and sometimes through programming of their own). Generally, community chests work toward poverty alleviation, but they can sometimes have more specific missions. Community chests gained popularity in the nineteenth and twentieth centuries, as citizens needed a more formalized way to give back to their communities beyond neighbor-to-neighbor contributions.

Foundations—The Good, the Bad, and the Controversial

A foundation is a type of nonprofit organization that is created from designated funds that then distributes these funds out to organizations or people in the form of grants. Sometimes foundations can be exclusively grant-makers, and sometimes foundations also have their own affiliated philanthropic programs that work in conjunction with the nonprofit recipients of their grants. Normally, foundations are formed with private wealth from an individual, family, or corporation that is established with charitable intent. Funds are usually held in what's called an endowment, which is typically not supposed to be spent but is invested so that it generates income. This allows foundations to exist for decades at a time, but by law, foundations are required to distribute/spend at least 5 percent of their investment interest on charitable purposes.

There are four types of foundations:

- *Independent Foundations*—Organizations founded with private wealth to aid charitable purposes, often established by a wealthy individual or family.
- *Corporate Foundations*—A corporation can set aside a chunk of its wealth into a sister foundation that gives grants to nonprofit organizations on behalf of the corporation.
- *Operating Foundations*—These foundations are unique in that they use their resources exclusively to provide a direct service for a nonprofit organization. These are typically research-driven or support museums.
- *Community Foundations*—Community trusts and foundations make grants for social purposes in one specific region that they serve. Unlike the other types of foundations, these operate using public funds rather than private wealth.

Foundations have technically been around for centuries. For example, the library at Alexandria was technically considered a foundation, as was Plato's Academy in Greece. It was not until the twentieth century, however, that foundational grants were able to make widespread changes to society and foundations were considered an established form of nonprofit organization. In the early twentieth century, in the wake of the Industrial Revolution, science and reason were held in higher esteem than ever before. People began to seek forms of giving that were less sentimental, religious, or driven by emotional altruism. Foundations sought to have a long-lasting impact on society as a whole, rather than impact one person or a group of people.

This concept was known as Scientific Philanthropy and predominantly used research to address the root cause of an issue. Staying true to this concept, most foundations today are still more businesslike in their operations and more methodical in their evaluation of the grantee's impact on society. Clearly, foundations have had a huge impact on American history and continue to do so today. Notably, the Bill and Melinda Gates Foundation has one of the most thorough application and reporting process with its grantees, and because of this the foundation made incredible strides in wiping malaria off the face of the planet in a very short time.

How Do You Apply for Foundation Grants?

Each foundation has a slightly different process for granting to nonprofit organizations. Some of the larger foundations, such as the Gates Foundation, contact organizations directly with whom they are interested in partnering. Normally, nonprofit organizations apply for grants using an RFP (request for proposal), and they are posted on the foundation's website as well as on grant-searching sites. These requests outline the mission of the foundation's grant and detail the kind of information they require from the nonprofit. This often includes tax returns, annual reports, reports on the nonprofit's success with metrics, and a detailed summary of their intended use for the grant. Often, the foundation will also ask for accounts of what the nonprofit will do if they are *not* granted this money. This is because a well-supported organization with diversified funding is much more attractive to a foundation. More often than not, foundations want to know that the applying nonprofit could stand on its own without their money.

If you are interested in learning more about the foundation granting process, there are several online courses you can take. The most notable of these is called Giving with Purpose, a Google+ supported online course that is open to the public. In this course, put forth by the Learning by Giving Foundation (founded by Doris Buffet), you can learn about the grantee process and you and your classmates will ultimately decide on local charities to receive grants from Ms. Buffet herself.

There are three main functions of foundations: *driver, partner,* and *catalyst.* When a social goal can be clearly mapped and planned by a foundation, it acts as a *driver* and makes grants to organizations that will carry out the plan and strategy devised by the foundation. When foundations share power with their grantee organizations and decisions are made together, the foundation acts as a *partner.* In the role of *catalyst,* a foundation relies on the grantee nonprofit organization to develop and execute a plan to solve said social issue.

There are some, however, that do not believe foundations should exist in perpetuity. It was Andrew Carnegie himself, considered the father of American philanthropy, who said, "He who dies wealthy dies disgraced" and "a dollar saved is a stinking fish." Many believe that if foundations gave more resources away, a plethora of worldwide social issues could be solved. However, because only 5 percent of a foundation's wealth *must* be given away annually by law, there are many foundations that only grant the bare minimum required to maintain their nonprofit status. In fact, some modern critics accuse foundations, predominantly family foundations, with starting their organizations as a way to evade taxes and protect their own wealth. After all, giving away only 5 percent of funds per year retains far more of one's wealth in the long run than paying the current income tax rate. To combat this, many (including Bill and Melinda Gates, Warren Buffet, and George Lucas) have entered into the "Giving Club" that brings in the wealthiest philanthropists of our day and requires that they pledge to give away the majority of their wealth to philanthropic purposes before they die.

Andrew Carnegie—America's Favorite Philanthropist?

Born into poverty in Scotland, Carnegie is an interesting study in American philanthropic tradition. He made his fortune in the steel industry and believed that the rich had a duty to care for the poor. Carnegie developed a passion for reading books at an early age and was responsible for the creation of three thousand libraries around the country to further promote his belief that all people had the right to a quality education. He also endowed the Carnegie Corporation in New York in 1911, which still exists to "promote the advancement and diffusion of knowledge and understanding." However, Andrew Carnegie was notorious for keeping his workers in poverty by paying them a very poor wage and forcing them to work in unsafe conditions—all to keep himself wealthy. In fact, his wage cuts even resulted in violent strikes in 1892. While he is known as one of the most successful figures in American capitalism and philanthropy, was he truly deserving of that title? Had he paid his workers a decent wage and offered them benefits, would he have improved society as much or perhaps more than he did by bestowing mass wealth on those who did not work for him? We will never know, but there are many things to consider when looking at wealthy, business-driven giving.

"Grassroots" Charities and Their Importance in the Sector

Even though there are millions of nonprofit organizations in the United States, not all of them are accounted for. Not all nonprofits are required to register with the IRS, which skews official counts. Religious organizations and congregations are not required to register with the IRS, nor are smaller organizations that make less than $25,000 of annual revenue. However, any organization that makes less than $500,000 a year is defined as "grassroots." Grassroots organizations, while small in size, play an incredibly important part in the overall sector.

More than half of the nonprofit organizations in the United States are considered grassroots. These organizations are typically run by a team of volunteers and/or a governing board, as they rarely have full-time paid staff. Furthermore, their funding is most likely comprised of individual donations rather than large corporate, foundational, or governmental grants. Grassroots sources of funding can also include events that are usually smaller in scale but still generate revenue thanks to donated venues, goods, and services. Marketing for grassroots organizations is also almost exclusively via word-of-mouth, social media, e-mail, or posters around their communities. Internet marketing/fund-raising, public speaking events, and personal solicitations are also impactful sources of revenue when the nonprofit has the means to participate. This highly personalized approach of advertising and advocating for grassroots charities can help grassroots charities to grow exponentially.

Mutual Benefit Societies

Another type of tax-exempt nonprofit is mutual benefit organizations that focus on reciprocal philanthropy. These are generally defined as organizations that are established primarily to serve the members of a particular group of people. Examples of these would be the NAACP (National Association for the Advancement of Colored People) or the American Bar Association. These groups have been extremely integral to American democracy, as these are some of the oldest and most successful philanthropic organizations that protect and advance disadvantaged groups such as women or minorities. For example, in 1866 in the wake of the Civil War, the Female Mutual Relief Society was formed. It gave working women sickness insurance as well as a one dollar per week salary to avoid homeless shelters and reliance on charity. Before mutual benefit societies, insurance was not a normative concept. This led to a huge rise in mutual benefit associations and fraternities in the late nineteenth and early twentieth centuries. Once insurance became privatized, the number of fraternities and mutual benefit organizations began to decline.

Members of mutual benefit societies and organizations also benefit from the social capital gained from membership. Job opportunities, civic engagement prospects, and personal connections all spring from being in a formalized agency with a common goal of self-help and reciprocated acts of charity.

What Does It Take to Be a Nonprofit?

The application process for receiving nonprofit status varies by state. However, the steps are generally the same. First, one needs to establish a nonprofit corporation by filing the Articles of Incorporation. Parts of this initial process usually include: obtaining a federal tax ID (FEIN) from the IRS, the preparation of bylaws and the governance rules that the organization's board of directors must follow. After this is done, obtaining a 501(c)(3) status becomes more complicated. To obtain this status, you must apply to the IRS for recognition of tax exemption by filing the IRS form 1023. This is a long process (up to twenty-eight pages of forms) with required attachments such as an audit of a tax return, examination of an organization's internal governing structure, financial records, purposes, and planned programs. The IRS also looks for conflicts of interest on their governing boards and potential benefit to insiders. See Appendix B for details.

Then, one must complete the Charitable Solicitations Registrations, which is a requirement in forty states and is usually administered by the Attorney General's office. In some cases they must apply for state corporate tax exemption. Most states recognize federal tax exemption as valid, but this varies by state. Lastly, many states grant nonprofits a state sales tax exemption, which allows organizations to purchase items for use by their organization without having to pay sales tax.

This whole process can be quick or slow, depending on the size and structure of the organization and the state in which they reside. However, it is all 100 percent vital to having a successful, reputable nonprofit organization.

501(c)(4) Organizations

501(c)(4) organizations are the second largest nonprofit category. These are defined as "Civic leagues, social welfare organizations, and local associations of employees," which can encapsulate several kinds of organizations—and it is meant to. The biggest difference between 501(c)(3)s and 501(c)(4)s is that the latter *can participate in and raise money for political activities*. Organizations defined as "social welfare" organizations are also a part of this category, which includes service clubs. Examples of this are organizations like Lion's Club or the Rotary Club, which provide networking and communion among their members and give back to their communities through volunteerism.

The IRS is very strict about 501(c)(3)s being politically active, and this is one of the biggest reasons that nonprofits lose their tax-exempt status. The IRS considers the following activities to qualify as a "political activity" of a 501(c)(3), according to NOLO Online Legal forums:

- Inviting a political candidate to make a campaign speech at an event hosted by the organization
- Using the organization's funds to publish materials that support (or oppose) a candidate

- Donating money from the organization to a political candidate
- Any statements by the organization's executive director, in his or her official capacity, that support a candidate
- Criticizing or supporting a candidate on the organization's website
- Inviting one candidate to speak at a well-publicized and well-attended event, and inviting the other candidate to speak at a lesser function
- Inviting all candidates to speak at an event, but arranging the speaking event or choosing the questions in such a way that it is obvious that the organization favors one candidate over the others
- Conducting a "get out the vote" telephone drive in a partisan manner by selecting caller responses for further follow-up based on candidate preference
- Using the organization's website to link to only one candidate's profile

Nonprofit Revenue Sources

Many people believe that nonprofit organizations rely solely on donations to keep themselves financially afloat; however, this is not the case at all. The majority of nonprofit income is generated from fees for services or goods from private sources and government. "Fees for services" include things like ticket sales, membership fees, payments for services, and tuition to nonprofit universities. Government grants are also a large source of income, as are investment incomes like the foundation endowments we discussed earlier in the chapter. Only 13 percent of nonprofit income comes from private contributions.

Of these private contributions, the majority (71 percent) is generated by individual donations from private citizens. Grant-making foundations then account for about 16 percent of revenue, followed by bequests and legacy giving, at 9 percent. Corporations, despite having the capacity to give vast amounts, only account for about 5 percent of nonprofit donations.

Source: Giving USA Report 2015

Government grants are also another source of income for nonprofits. Many state and federal offices have the funding and the intent to implement social programs in their areas but do not have the know-how to do so. Often they will grant money to and entrust nonprofit organizations to implement these programs. mostly health and educational. However, there is some concern among nonprofits that there may be strings attached to these dollars. In many cases, nonprofits have to modify or entirely restructure their programming in order to receive government funding, which raises concerns among nonprofit donors and managerial staff about the merits of choosing this funding option.

Foundations, as covered above, are another source of funding and account for 16 percent of revenue.

Corporations are the biggest 'wild card' when it comes to nonprofit funding. Many corporations have 'sister' foundations, where profits from the company get siphoned into the foundation to be granted out to nonprofits. Sometimes the gift comes from the corporation itself, which may have the purpose of increasing its visibility and esteem in a community. Corporation giving is at an all-time high, even though it is only about 5 percent of nonprofit funding, as consumers are increasingly interested in the charitable giving practices of for-profit businesses. More customers are demanding that businesses be socially minded and generous. However, even if a corporation does not give direct dollars to a nonprofit organization, they can also be charitable through their practices and products. This concept is called *philanthrocapitalism*. There are a few ways that businesses engage in this concept; the most notable example is that of the RED brand. The Gap's RED campaign started small. Part of the proceeds for certain clothing items in their store went toward AIDS research and alleviation in Africa. Many celebrities got involved in this campaign, including Oprah Winfrey and Bono, which increased its popularity and visibility. This campaign eventually spread to several other brands, and Product RED is now a household name.

Nonprofit MYTH BUSTER—"Nonprofits are not as structured and businesslike as the private sector."

> Now, more than ever, nonprofit organizations are approaching their work with businesslike strategies. More colleges and universities offer degrees in nonprofit management, public good, and philanthropy, which primes a new generation of nonprofit workers to make a difference in an intelligent, strategic way. Well-run nonprofits are structured, accountable, and efficient using the same (or similar) approaches that for-profit businesses use to maximize their effectiveness. Because nonprofits generally do not have the same large budgets as for-profits, nonprofit management teams utilize

even *more* cost-cutting, time-saving and resource-maximizing tactics than their for-profit counterparts.

Why Do Nonprofits Exist?

The United States has a strong nonprofit sector and volunteer presence for one main reason—we *need* it. This sector enables us to achieve more public benefit without specific constraints that are put upon the governmental or private business sectors. The nonprofit sector allows for experimentation (such as low-cost and low-risk social research/development), has freedom from governmental bureaucracies (red tape), and provides attention to people and/or needs that the majority may overlook. Famed French political scientist and diplomat Alexis de Tocqueville described American associations as a way for citizens to escape the 'tyranny of the majority' that controls our democratic process in his 1835 publication *Democracy in America.*

There are a few formalized theories as to why nonprofits exist and thrive today. One of these, developed in 1973 by Krashinsky, is called the "market failure" theory. In situations where a consumer is unable to fully evaluate the quality and effectiveness of a for-profit product or service, nonprofits arise to fulfill this consumer's need, as they have little to no incentives to cut costs in order to maximize profits. Another theory is called "governance failure," and it states that nonprofits fulfill needs of society that do not have sufficient voter support. There are public goods that are sometimes desired by some, but not the majority of citizens, and philanthropy fulfills their unsatisfied demands.

A more simplistic and often-cited theory for why nonprofits exist and thrive is called the "trust theory." In short, nonprofits are preferred to provide goods and services over government or private business sources because they are bound by nondistribution constraints and are not driven by wealth and profit. Where there is imperfect, incomplete, or inconsistent information provided by governmental sources and businesses, there is a lack of trust. Therefore, nonprofits will be chosen as the most "trustworthy" vehicle to provide social goods and services.

What Do People Give to Nonprofits?

People often only associate money with philanthropy, as the traditional notion of philanthropy is centered around monetary transactions. However, there are many things one can give to a nonprofit that are just as (if not more) valuable than money.

As mentioned previously, nonprofit contributions are generally divided into *time, talent, and treasure*.

> Time (Volunteerism)
> The civic health of any community is dependent on volunteering, and Americans *love* to volunteer. In 2013, 62.6 million adults (about one-fourth of the population) volunteered through a nonprofit organization. This resulted in about 7.7 billion volunteer hours, and the estimated value of this service was about $173 billion dollars (based on the third sector's estimated value of a volunteer hour). Of course, even more people participated in informal volunteering in their communities—138 million Americans. This includes helping neighbors, watching each other's children, house-sitting, and so on. Volunteer service, whether formal or informal, does more than help nonprofits—it helps increase the civic health and well-being of communities, which vastly improves the quality of life of their residents.
>
> Talent (Skills)
> Donating one's skills to a nonprofit can be just as good as donating money. If your career afforded you a variety of sought-after skills

that can be useful to a nonprofit, make it known! This will save nonprofits time and money, where they would have otherwise had to hire or call upon an outside source. Volunteering your talents can also lead to exciting new opportunities such as part-time work, new hobbies, and an organizational relationship with a nonprofit that you can get involved in in other capacities (such as serving on its board).

Treasure (Money)

Of course, giving money to a nonprofit is the best no-muss-no-fuss way to contribute to the nonprofit sector. One can give unrestricted money directly (in the form of cash, check, or online donation), but one can also give "designated funds." This means that you want the organization to use your money in a specific way. An example of this would be giving to Big Brothers Big Sisters to support a specific pair of Bigs and Littles. Or, this could mean you want your money to go specifically toward operational or programming costs. You can also give money-garnering items, such as stocks. This will help a nonprofit organization build its endowment and have a stable base of income.

Who Gives to Nonprofits?

Nonprofit donors span every age, gender, ethnicity, and race across the United States. In short, *everyone* gives to nonprofit organizations. However, groups of different populations tend to give differently. It is difficult (and dangerous) to make broad generalizations about gender or race-based giving, but there are several trends that can be seen among different groups that are culturally relevant and fascinating. The amount of giving by diverse populations in this country is fairly consistent across the board; however, the *ways* in which they give tend to differ. It is important to recognize and be sensitive to cultural differences when engaging others in the philanthropic sphere.

Women in Philanthropy

The twenty-first century has witnessed huge strides for women in philanthropy. Thanks to the near-doubling of women in the workforce (from 29 percent in 1950 to 59 percent in 2007), women now have the means and power to give philanthropically at a very high level. Increases in employment, political power, and college degrees (particularly advanced and graduate degrees) indicate that women are no longer a minority audience but a part of the main populace.

Research done at the Women's Philanthropy Institute suggests that women's philanthropic habits, underlying motivations, and outcomes are significantly different from men's. Social and family dynamics impact how women and men grow up, which means that they differ in the way that they seek to impact their community through philanthropy. According to the research, men's and women's philanthropic habits differ in volunteerism, donor motivations, and influence.

The volunteer habits of women show that women volunteer significantly more than men do, especially single females, who, on average, volunteer 18 percent more than single men do. The unpublished dissertation "Women's Philanthropy: Motivations for Giving," by P. H. Parsons, shows that women who volunteer are more likely to provide fiscal support to organizations where they or their close friends and family spend volunteer time. Women provide many levels of organizational support beyond donations of money, including board participation and vast network connections that can advance a nonprofit forward greatly.

The Women's Philanthropy Institute, while studying donor motivations, discovered that women scored higher on "empathetic concern." This means that women typically feel more concern and protection for those in need. They also discovered that the top two donor motivations for women donors are "identifying with a certain cause" and "helping individuals meet their basic needs." The motivations of women and men in these groups also varied drastically by age, and in fact Silent Generation (born in 1945 or earlier) and Baby Boomer women are more likely to give to charity than all other age and gender groups. In this study, Millennial men were the least likely to give to charitable organizations. However, Millennials have yet to reach their peak earning potential, while those of the Silent Generation and Baby Boomers are in their prime philanthropic giving age.

Differences in gendered giving also vary by marital status. Eleanor Brown in her 2005 article "Married couples' charitable giving: Who and why" concluded that gifts are more likely to go to health, education, and religious organizations when the wife is the sole decision-maker (as opposed to when the two are joint decision-makers or when the husband decides). It was also found that when women make the philanthropic decisions, smaller amounts are given to *more* charities. Patrick Rooney, Eleanor Brown, and Debra Mesch (2007) also found that in households where women make the philanthropic decisions (or give separately from their husbands in general), they are more likely to give to educational causes. Women also generally live about 5.2 years longer than their male counterparts, so legacy giving and bequests can be very female-dominated.

Diverse Groups and Philanthropy

Hispanics or Latinos are diverse in their cultural traditions, as they hail from quite a few different countries all over the world. One overarching theme is that Latinos tend to give to religious institutions or mutual-assistance groups in their communities and give relatively little to conventional large charities. Latinos also engage in one-to-one philanthropy by sending money to their families and relatives outside the United States.

African Americans have a rich philanthropic tradition in the United States, particularly when it comes to inciting positive social change. According to Carson (1993), African Americans don't often view their actions as "philanthropy," as they tend to help more informally in their families and neighborhoods. While the informal assistance to family and friends remains the largest area of African American philanthropy, other predominant areas include religion, education, civil rights, youth programs, health care, and community economic development. A large motivation for philanthropy among this community is lifting up other African Americans, making it a wonderful example of how philanthropy can change the culture, view, and policies of a nation. African American philanthropy is fluid; it changes and adapts as the social climate in America does.

There are more than forty distinct ethnic groups among Asian Americans and Pacific Islanders, and their philanthropic traditions are just as diverse. However, some overarching trends include: mutual aid societies, family, self-help groups, education, and long-term health care for the elderly. There are strong ties between philanthropy and debt in the Asian American community, as many see philanthropy as a way to pay back their debts to their families and communities. Age tends to be a significant factor in how the Asian American population chooses to give, as well as the length of time they have been in the United States. Those who have had several generations before them living in the United States tend to give more traditionally through larger non-profit organizations.

Native American communities had guidelines and philanthropic traditions long before European influence on Western culture. Giving was a way of life rather than an obligation, and the focus was on the *spirit* of the gift (rather than on the value of the gift). Moreover, all giving was interconnected, which made both the giving of a gift and the receiving of a gift a distinct honor. Modern Native American giving tends to focus on the preservation of the environment, ensuring racial equality, cultural preservation, health care, and support of rural communities. Something distinct to the Native American community is that members prefer to make need-based, anonymous donations more than other groups of individuals.

Arab Americans are another diverse group, as they are influenced by several different religious traditions and geographical traditions. Like other groups, Arab Americans tend to give emotionally rather than for formal tax purposes or for recognition. Arab Americans tend to donate to mosques and churches or send money back to their relatives in other countries before donating to a US nonprofit organization. It is the community's cherished traditions that influence their philanthropy within the United States. Most often, these traditions hail from the Middle East, North Africa, their own families, or community/religious tradition.

Philanthropy by the Numbers—Differences in Age Groups

While there is much debate as to when one generation ends and another begins, there are general guidelines used to define generations (even though these lines get somewhat blurred):

- Silent Generation—born in 1945 or earlier
- Boomers—born 1946 to 1964
- Generation X—born 1965 to 1980 (although some end this generation at 1976)
- Millennials—born 1980 to 2000

Charitable giving is often dependent upon household income, which varies greatly by which generations live together under one roof. Boomers account for the largest amount of households (44 million) in the United States as of 2009. They also have the largest number of households with net incomes above $75,000. Generation X is in second place, with 34.3 million households, 11.5 million of which have incomes over $75,000. In third place is the Silent Generation, with 24.4 million households and 5.9 million with $75,000 or more. Generation X and Millennials have about 13 million households with net income over $75,000 which indicates that they will soon be coming into leadership roles and will be entering their peak earning years, making them the future of philanthropy.

The book *Achieving Excellence in Fundraising* says that one needs to consider the difference between *cohort* effects and *lifestyle* effects. Cohort effect is the characteristic of people in the group throughout their lives. Going through large life events (they cite the Great Depression as an example) may change one's attitude toward money, scarcity, and philanthropy permanently. However, lifestyle effect changes as people age. A person in his or her forties may give differently than he or she did twenty years ago due to income levels, devotion to different causes, or general status in life.

After defining these, we can examine the essential differences in how generations give. While the probability of charitable gifts and amount given is lower for Millennials, they give a larger percentage of their income than the Boomers and Silent Generation. Generation X also gives less than Boomers, but they are just as likely to give as Boomers. The largest deterrent to charitable giving cited by Generation Xers and Millennials are financial hardships such as bills, debts, and cost of education and living—and this was *before* the economic crash of 2008.

There are several generational differences in motivations for giving as well.

Silent Generation

This generation is generally phasing out their professional life and gearing up for retirement, if they aren't already retired. Many of them will work part time or as consultants and have reported having stronger than normal feelings of loyalty for charitable organizations they have supported in the past. Their "responsibility to give" is cited as the number one reason for their charitable contributions, and they report wanting to help people meet basic needs and "help people help themselves" as motivators.

Boomers

Baby Boomers are still a dominant economic force in the United States and international landscape. While Boomers are less likely to be donors than the Silent Generation, their average giving total is not very different from that of Silent Generation households. Boomers are more likely to support educational causes than the Silent Generation but less likely to support health-related causes. Boomer women in particular top the charts in likelihood of giving and have emerged as a formidable economic force in philanthropy.

Generation X

While Gen-Xers do not have as many members as Boomers or Millennials, they have distinguished their giving patterns through nontraditional ways of giving back (such as the emergence of social entrepreneurs.) Generation X and Boomers are similarly likely to make a gift, but they give less on average per household. Generation X's priorities include health and human services, but they give less to educational causes.

Millennials

While they may be an easy target for scrutiny and criticism, there are an estimated sixty million Millennials, so their giving patterns do in fact matter for the future of philanthropy. Their motivations for giving are distinctly different, as focus groups cited "wanting to change the world" as their number one motivation for giving. However the majority of Millennials have not yet reached their peak earning potential and give back in other ways (such as organizational volunteering), as they are more comfortable working in groups more than any other generation. Also, they appreciate having more opportunity to plan an active role in organizational decision-making, rather than implementing others' ideas.

How Do I Get Started?

There are a plethora of tools and resources that you can use to research nonprofit organizations and find the one to support that best suits your needs. Websites such as Guidestar or Charity Navigator evaluate nonprofit organizations based on several aspects, such as effectiveness, stewardship of donations, efficiency, and so on. For example, Charity Navigator defines the following criteria for assigning a charitable organization's score on its website:

1. Tax Status: The organization must be registered as a 501(c)(3) public charity and must file a Form 990.

2. Revenue: The charity must have generated at least $1 million in revenue for two consecutive years.
3. Length of Operations: The organization must have been in existence, with corresponding Forms 990, for at least seven years.
4. Location: While we only rate charities based in the United States and registered with the IRS, the scope of a charity's work can be international. In fact, we rate more than a thousand charities that have an international aspect to their work.
5. Public Support: The charity must have at least $500,000 in public support. Public support must account for at least 40 percent of total revenue for at least two consecutive years.
6. Fund-raising Expenses: The charity must have at least 1 percent of its expenses allocated to fund-raising for three consecutive years.
7. Administrative Expenses: The charity must have at least 1 percent of its expenses allocated to administrative expense for three consecutive years.

Charity Navigator and other "watchdog" websites must also be scrutinized, because they too come with different sets of beliefs, priorities, and biases.

Websites of charitable organizations also provide extremely helpful information, along with popular media sources such as Facebook and local publications. There are also specialized academic publications, including *Nonprofit Quarterly* or *Chronicle of Philanthropy* that will keep you up to date on nonprofit news, trends, successes, and failures within the field as well as cutting-edge philanthropic research.

Nonprofit Employees

About 11 million people in the United States are currently employed by nonprofits. The nonprofit sector also succeeds in employing more people than agriculture, mining, construction, transportation, communication, finance, insurance, and real estate combined. People have successfully built meaningful and successful careers in the nonprofit sector, and that is because it offers distinct advantages to its employees. For example, knowing you are contributing to social benefit makes work fulfilling and satisfying. There has also been evidence that nonprofit workers have a better work/life balance; in large part, this is attributed to the fact that managerial staff at nonprofits often understand the need workers have for flexibility and compassion as a normative element of their work structure. Nonprofit employees are offered annual salaries anywhere from $22,000 to nearly $800,000 per year, depending on skill level, experience, position, and organizational budget. While nonprofit salaries (particularly that of a CEO or high-level manager) are a touchy subject, especially in the media, it is important to remember a few things:

1. Nonprofit workers deserve a living wage, just as anyone working in the private or governmental sector does.
2. Just because they're doing altruistic work does not mean they are not deserving of compensation for their time and talents that is reflective of the quality and impact of their work.

Nonprofit MYTH BUSTER—"Nonprofit workers should not make much money; they should do it for the joy of giving back to society."

One of the most damaging myths about the nonprofit sector is that nonprofit workers should be doing this work out of the goodness of their hearts and should not receive compensation for their work that is comparable to private sector jobs. Nonprofits have a serious role in changing the world, and often society frowns upon nonprofit workers making livable wages. Author Dan Pallotta has famously called out this disconnect between how we view charitable action and the work that they do. Often there is a double standard where nonprofits are rewarded and celebrated for how little they spend—and not for their impact upon the world we live in. Americans often equate frugality with morality, and the concept that altruism is its own reward drives many peoples' thoughts about the nonprofit sector. Pallotta challenges us to start rewarding charities for their big goals and big accomplishments, even when they come with big expenses, as that is the only way to truly create systemic changes in our nation.

In short, nonprofits have continuously grown in size and revenue for decades, including through recessions and times of political strife. This sector of society can continuously do the work that either cannot or will not be done by the government or businesses. It is comforting to know that nonprofits have a societal benefit as their main objective—not money or power—and therefore that is why most people trust nonprofits to do good, honest, and transparent work. Nonprofits perfectly demonstrate one of the most vital components of our democracy: pluralism. When there is a group that is unrepresented (or underrepresented) in government, nonprofits allow for that group's voice to be heard in an impactful way free of tyranny. This is why the nonprofit support is vital even today, as there will always be marginalized groups that deserve equality, justice, and representation in America.

CHAPTER 6

New Mediums of Giving

In the twenty-first century, people have many ways of giving instead of the traditional year-end check writing to your favorite charity, which was the norm in the twentieth century. Many nonprofit organizations have transitioned to these kinds of giving when they solicit donors. My local public radio station has cut the duration of its pledge drives during the year by adopting online payment and sustained giving over many years. Other forms of giving include crowdfunding, microfinance programs, philanthrocapitalism, and social entrepreneurship. By using the various forms of fundraising, nonprofits serving the poor and needy can get the required funds for their success and survival.

Crowdfunding

This method of giving throws a wide net for potential donors who are empathetic to the cause. The number of contributors is large, with donations varying from ten dollars to more than one hundred. The essentials for this to be successful include

1. a good website that describes the cause in an attractive manner and makes it easy to donate;

2. a large mailing list of potential donors in the area where the cause is located, or of donors who will be attracted to the cause; and
3. a campaign of sending out e-mails and follow up e-mails to raise the funds.

Donors must be acknowledged through receipts and informed as to how the funds were used.

The top crowdfunding sites by volume are:

1. GoFundMe
2. Kickstarter
3. Indiegogo
4. Teespring
5. Patreon
6. YouCaring
7. CrowdRise
8. DonorsChoose
9. Kiva
10. GiveForward

According to Entrepreneur.com, there are several keys to successful crowdfunding. First, Listen to your audience. Having a great idea doesn't necessarily mean it will make millions of dollars. The best way to make sure your idea will be successful is to ask anyone and everyone's opinion of it. Social media is a great way to get opinions on your product—both positive and negative. By listening to the people who will purchase your product, you can take this criticism and make improvements before you release it to the masses.

Do product testing. Create a team that can test your product extensively. This will find the errors and mistakes and build a better product. You want to suss this out before you ship it to your online customers.

Next, don't make promises you can't keep. This is a surefire way to make your customers angry, and you'll end up with bad reviews.

Build trust and be as informative as you can. An informative, well-written paragraph on your page is key. This is how you will educate and inform your customer, so the more details you include, the better.

Finally, create a great video. Crowdfunding projects that include a video sell 50 percent more than projects without a video. This engages your customer with your product and makes them more excited to purchase it.

Microfinancing

We all have heard of Kiva.org (made popular by President Clinton), or Grameen Bank (founded by Mohammed Younus of Bangladesh). Through these microfinance organizations, anyone can give a loan as small as twenty-five dollars to help the poor improve their life. The impact of these small loans is considerable and has given birth to a lot of small entrepreneurs in the developing world. The amazing thing about microfinance loans is that the repayment rate for them is as high as 98 percent. The person who takes a small loan will repay it and then get a bigger loan and expand his or her business. Microfinancing has eliminated dire poverty in many parts of the world, and now big banks give loans to microfinance lending agencies—the scope for microfinance loans is continuously expanding.

The power of any individual to help his or her fellow human being is amply demonstrated by the microfinance model. When Mohammed Younus, a professor in the United States originally from Bangladesh, found out that poor people in Dhaka could not get a loan to start their own small business, he loaned his own money to a few and realized that these people are eager to repay their loan and take out a bigger loan to expand their business. Now, the company Younus started, Grameen Bank, is a multibillion dollar company that helps millions of people come out of poverty through its microfinance programs.

Here are a few microfinance success stories from the Microloan Foundation in the United Kingdom (taken from microloanfoundation.org):

- "My name is Christabel Mwansa Muntunga. I'm forty-six and a widow. I'm the treasurer for Tiyeseko woman credit group in Kafue Zambia. *Tiyeseko* means 'We Are Trying.' I'm a mother of four and live in a two room house with my two children and two grandchildren.

    "When my husband died in 2012, his relatives grabbed all of our properties and my life become unbearable. Since my husband's death, none of my relatives and my late husband's relatives helped me financially. I received a loan from microloan last year, my children and I used to struggle, back then we only used to eat lunch and supper. Since I got a loan from microloan, I'm able to provide three meals a day for my children and they don't miss school anymore.

    "I have been with microloan for over a year. I started with k700 (£57) and used to make a profit of k150 (£12), but now I only make a profit of k120 (£10) due to slow business in the country as of now.

    "I have learned how to calculate my cost, profit, loss, and saving. I have expanded my business and order more goods to re-sell. I have a free mind and don't worry too much about whether I'm making a loss or not. I'm able to work at my own time and not beg for handouts. My future plans are to educate my children up to college through profits made at this business."

- "Margaret is a very smartly dressed lady. Her customers would expect no less, because Margaret's business is selling secondhand clothing. The dresses, shirts, coats, and other garments come in to Lilongwe, the capital of Malawi, from all over the world. Once a fortnight, Margaret travels to Lilongwe to replenish her stock, and then travels around local village markets selling the clothes. Margaret's business was made possible six years ago, when she first started working with MicroLoan.

    "Like other women we support, Margaret has a real entrepreneurial spirit. As Malawi experiences very heavy rains for several months of the year, making it almost impossible to travel, Margaret has set up a second business thanks to additional loans from MicroLoan. Margaret's second business is a small grocery shop near her home, where she sells charcoal, tomatoes, and other fruits and vegetables. By diversifying her income in this way, Margaret is protecting herself and her four children, providing the best opportunity to live a sustainable life free from difficulty. This is the kind of business knowledge that MicroLoan clients are taught as part of their ongoing training. It proves invaluable.

    "But not even two businesses are enough for Margaret. Using the profits from her businesses, she has started building small houses on the land surrounding her home. Margaret rents out four of the houses she has built, bringing in over £21 per month. This would never have been possible without MicroLoan's support.

    "When you add in the ducks, chickens, and pigs that she keeps for eating and selling, you can see how well established Margaret really is."

- "Joyce is fairly new to MicroLoan; she is in the middle of her second loan cycle. Before Joyce knew about MicroLoan Foundation, like most other rural Malawians, she and her husband Hashim were subsistence farmers. They had a small patch of land and just about produced enough maize and cassava to feed their four children and themselves. When Joyce heard about MicroLoan Foundation, she applied for a loan to set up a small shop in the village where she would sell tea and bread. Like many of the women we work with, Joyce is lucky to have her husband's support in her business ventures. Hashim buys the bread from a market five miles away, bringing back about twenty loaves each day on his bicycle. Meanwhile, Joyce brews the tea and looks after the shop.

Joyce acknowledges the importance of education; she stayed at primary school until she was nearly eighteen years old so that she could read, write, and count properly. Today, she is an eager participant in the group training sessions led by Richard, the MicroLoan Branch Manager. The group sessions are a joyous occasion, starting and ending with singing and dancing.

"It is still early days for Joyce and Hashim, and there are many ways in which she might choose to develop her business to increase profits; she might start baking her own bread or expand the range of products she sells in the shop.

"At the moment though, Joyce and Hashim are enjoying the business and are saving money so they can build a larger house to fit their family more comfortably."

Philanthrocapitalism

The twenty-first century has given rise to a new word in our vocabulary: *philanthrocapitalism*. This is a significant expansion of how a few rich people gave away their wealth in the twentieth century in America, the most famous being Andrew Carnegie and John D. Rockefeller. As the Internet and financial sectors have expanded rapidly around the world, the capitalists who made money in these sectors have decided to use their business skills to help the poor through philanthrocapitalism. Matthew Bishop and Michael Green, in their 2008 book on philanthrocapitalism, state that giving by American foundations rose from $13.8 billion in 1996 to $31.6 billion in 2006. On June 26, 2006, Warren Buffet announced that he was giving away $37 billion to his children ($6 billion) and Bill Gates ($31 billion) so that they could give it away well through their charitable foundations. In May 2009, a meeting of the super-rich folks was held in New York City to discuss how to give away their money effectively in order to solve problems around the world. Warren Buffet and Bill Gates are now the champions for philanthrocapitalism and are recruiting many super-rich people to give away at least 50 percent of their wealth for public causes.

Philanthrocapitalism is spreading to other parts of the world. The Clinton Global Initiative, started by the Clinton Foundation in 2005, has been collecting world leaders and philanthropists to discuss how they can eliminate hunger and disease and improve educational quality around the world. In 2007, communications mogul Carlos Slim Helu of Mexico donated $10 billion to alleviate poverty in Mexico and Latin America. In 2011, Aziz Premji of India started his educational initiative to improve the quality of and access to good education all over India. Many other super-rich people around the world have started their own foundations and are transforming the lives of the poor in their part of the world.

The causes that the super-rich feel a responsibility to address generally start with personal experience (Bishop and Green, 2008). Michael Milliken has given $750 million to fight prostate cancer since he suffered from the disease. Alumni giving is based on this concept—alumni feel obligated to their university for their success and give big. Michael Bloomberg, Chuck Feeney, and Sandy Weill have given hundreds of millions of dollars to their alma maters. George Dees of Duke University states that "philanthrocapitalists mobilize and deploy private resources (time, talent, and treasure) to improve the world in which we live." Global Philanthropists Circle is an organization that helps wealthy families give more effectively.

Corporations engage in philanthrocapitalism in a big way. Sergey Brin and Larry Page of Google state, "We believe strongly that in the long term, we will be better served—as shareholders and in all other ways—by a company that does good things for the world, even if we forgo some short-term gains." The Indian government felt the need to pass a law in 2014 mandating that Indian corporations of a certain size must set aside 2 percent of their profits and account for this in their tax returns under the title of Corporate Social Responsibility (CSR) Fund. Some companies have started their own non-governmental organization (NGO) to utilize this fund, but many evaluate the requests for funding from the many NGOs in India and give grants for causes they believe in. Tata Sons, one of the oldest conglomerates in India, has maintained the Tata Foundation for many years and provides much more than the minimum required by the government. The line between company wealth and personal wealth is more blurred in developing countries, which makes the distinction between corporate and personal philanthropy less important for rich people in these countries (Bishop and Green, 2008).

In China, foreign companies have been members of the Global Business Coalition of HIV/AIDS, Tuberculosis, and Malaria and build good relations with the government by helping it tackle some of the country's social and health problems. American companies and foundations that have a lot of business contacts in India give a large amount of grants to nonprofits in the United States that are tackling the social problems in India. They also do a lot to alleviate poverty in India. The organization I headed in Chicago for many years, PrathamUSA, has significantly benefited from this trend and has made a significant impact on the education and skill-building needs of the poor in India.

Bishop and Green also talk about celebrity philanthropists (termed *celanthropist*), with people like Bono and Oprah Winfrey doing good around the world. They bring a mastery of branding, mass communication skills, and high-level access to further the causes they believe in. Angelina Jolie, Brad Pitt, and Princess Diana are other examples of celebrities who have teamed with governments and wealthy individuals to make huge impacts in impoverished countries and within the poor areas of the United States. In India, celebrity philanthropists are few, but I am sure that as they get comfortable with their wealth and celebrity, there will be more of them stepping up to improve poor communities in India.

Social Entrepreneurship
Social entrepreneurship is defined as a business that addresses the social needs of society while being financially and environmentally sustainable. Many retirees can use their business and technical skills to become social entrepreneurs and make a big impact on society while earning an income to supplement their social security and other savings. Alternatively, they can help established social entrepreneurs by giving their time and talent, and they can gain satisfaction from the impact they are making on societal needs. The American Association of Retired Persons (AARP) publishes a magazine that includes, among other topics, success stories of social entrepreneurs who are living fulfilled lives. The needs in your local community or in any part of the world you are interested in are many, and using social entrepreneurship and innovation, you can make a huge difference in the lives of many poor people.

Bishop and Green (2008) describe entrepreneurial philanthropists like Omidyar and Skoll of eBay who are supporting social entrepreneurs around the world. They became to embrace this idea by seeing the impact of a donation of a $1 million block of shares in their company to the Silicon Valley Community Foundation. The Foundation sold the shares a year later and realized $40 million for their social work. The annual Skoll Awards for Social

Entrepreneurship promotes the best social entrepreneurs in the US and has provided millions of dollars to these effective social entrepreneurs who are making a huge impact in the field s of education, world peace and other public causes. I was personally involved in a 2014 Skoll Challenge Grant and it made me reach out to donors to maximize what our nonprofit would receive from the Foundation.

One of the pioneers of Social Entrepreneurship has been Bill Drayton of the Ashoka Foundation. Ashoka, founded in 1978, is dedicated to finding and fostering social entrepreneurs worldwide and has become a favorite investment vehicle of some of the leading philanthrocapitalists, according to Bishop and Green (2008). Ashoka has supported many social entrepreneurs in India and these people have changed many lives and improved the safety net in India. According to Drayton, the four stages of a social entrepreneur are: apprenticeship, launch, takeoff, and maturity. To promote these entrepreneurs, Ashoka provides fellowships to budding entrepreneurs and starts the apprenticeship process. Many Ashoka fellows have launched social organizations, and I know of many in India that have matured and made a demonstrable impact on society.

Echoing Green, established in 1987 by partners of General Atlantic, a private equity firm, has supported nearly four hundred and fifty social enterprises, including Teach for America. Such funds provide the seed capital to social entrepreneurs, similar to how the Venture Capitalists provide seed capital for commercial businesses. Now, many foundations including the John D. and Catherine T. MacArthur Foundation, Hewlett Foundation, Schwab Foundation and the Kaufmann Foundation, provide funds to social entrepreneurs. These foundations and wealthy individuals have provided the social sector badly needed business rigor, including regular monitoring and reporting of the impacts of their work.

Bishop and Green (2008) state that philanthrocapitalists like Omidyar and Skoll have improved the process of allocating capital to social entrepreneurs, thereby enabling them to build substantial organizations that are making a large-scale social impact. One such organization that I have been involved is PrathamUSA, which has grown from educating thousands of poor children in Maharashtra, India, to millions all over the country. With seed funding from UNICEF and large grants from the Hewlett, Google, and Microsoft Foundations, they are transforming lives of poor children through quality elementary and secondary education and vocational training. With their Annual Survey of Education Report (ASER), they are forcing the government of India to measure the quality of education instead of just access to education. The ASER model is now being emulated by many countries in Asia and Africa and Mexico.

The microfinance revolution started by Muhammad Younus and his Grameen Bank in 1974 in Bangladesh is one of the best examples of social entrepreneurship. The funds from Grameen Bank are loaned to social entrepreneurs, and the track record of repayment of these small microloans is a phenomenal 98 percent. With the rise of microfinance, people have learned to take their families through small enterprises and not depend on the government for handouts. Large banks and wealthy individuals have started providing funds to microfinance organizations, and thus the microfinance industry has rapidly grown worldwide. Carlos Danel of Banco Compartamos, Mexico, has turned from nonprofit to profit and serves a lot of the working poor in Mexico. It has received a lot of support from philanthropists in Mexico and argues that the for-profit model can help achieve scale and drive social change (Bishop and Green, 2008).

Universities have started offering courses on social entrepreneurship and nonprofit management. It is a fast-growing sector of the economy in developing countries and is also helping the inner city population in the United

States. The involvement of philanthropists has energized the social entrepreneurship movement, and it is an avenue for people who want to donate funds to make a difference in the lives of the poorest people in the world. Kiva.org allows donations of as little as twenty-five dollars, which are aggregated to provide social entrepreneurs the seed capital to start small businesses and provide for the families as well as serve the needs of society.

CHAPTER 7

Fundraising

According to *Achieving Excellence in Fundraising*, the philosophy of raising money is as follows: "Fundraising is the gentle art of teaching people the joy of giving." Philanthropy is not just about an exchange of money; it's an expression of values (as discussed in earlier chapters). Therefore, it's important to give to an organization that aligns with your personal moral structure. Money should be graciously received and joyously given, and the best way to achieve this goal is to work with an organization's fund raisers to maximize your impact at whatever level you chose to give.

Fund raisers are rejected by many and are seen so often in a negative light, to the point where "fund-raising" is sometimes considered a dirty word. However, they do one of the most important jobs for any nonprofit. Like it or not, money translates very easily and seamlessly into impact. Some examples include:

- It takes about $2,000 to support one mentoring relationship (one Big and one Little) for one year at Big Brothers Big Sisters. This includes activities for the match to do together, professional support from a Match Support Specialist, background checks, and all costs

associated with maintaining this relationship. In the end, that mentoring relationship could result in much more positive outcomes for children, such as the pursuit of higher education and the avoidance of risky behaviors, and it may also have an immeasurable impact on the lives of both the Bigs and the Littles.
- Every dollar donated to No Kid Hungry translates into ten meals for kids who do not get enough to eat. Although costs and tactics vary by location, this ratio was taken from their work in Maryland, where they were able to distribute more than two hundred thousand meals to children in one summer.
- It takes between $5,000 and $7,500 to build a well through the charity water.org (depending on the method of water collection) that provides clean, drinkable water to a community of several hundred people. This then stems into other results such as better health and greater access to education (particularly for girls), and it will eventually lift their communities out of poverty.
- Ten dollars to HALO Animal Rescue buys a bed and a blanket for a rescue animal that will now have a safe, warm, and clean place to be rehabilitated, cared for, and readied for adoption. One hundred dollars to HALO (as well as many other shelters) microchips ten animals, ensuring that families find their lost pets, keeping them off the street.
- One hundred dollars to Doctors Without Borders buys three first-aid kits, twenty-four blankets, and ten surgical scissors for medical personal to provide communities that are hit hard by war and disease (such as Haiti and Pakistan) with basic emergency healthcare and relief.

So as you can see, money may seem like a very impersonal form of action, but it is essential to achieving the mission of any nonprofit. So more than likely, you will be contacted by a fund raiser or asked for money from organizations in your area or organizations you've supported in the past. After all, the number one reason people do not give money to a nonprofit or cause is simply "because they weren't asked." The worst thing the prospective donor can say is no, and because this is heard so often by fund raisers, there is certainly no ill will. Fund raisers only expect that people/organizations give if and when they *can* and don't expect you to go beyond your means and abilities!

Identifying Potential Donors

1. Trust

It's important to remember as a potential donor that the fund raiser's ultimate goal of the meeting is not just about getting a check from you. Fund-raising is less about money than it is about *relationship building*. The organization benefits the most if it engages you enough that you become a lifelong supporter that will give (in one way or another) in whatever capacity is most satisfying and comfortable for you. If you can only give five dollars a month, they will not be offended and should not pressure you! Fund raisers are people too, and they understand that prospective donors have limitations on their finances, time, and energy.

When building these relationships, the most important piece of the puzzle is *trust*. It is trust that will build an organization's esteem and increase its donations. A large portion of Americans have very little to no trust in nonprofit organizations. This could be for all sorts of reasons, but it is most likely due to the media. The media loves to sensationalize stories about nonprofit scandals, mismanagement, and financial irresponsibility. It is important to remember that this is the exception, *not the rule*, but nevertheless, these stories really affect people's confidence in the nonprofit sector. Building trusting relationships with fund raisers and nonprofit organizations as a whole can not only increase your quality of life but can also raise the general public's esteem for nonprofit organizations' ability to enact change.

To illustrate this point, here is an example from Rajaram:

Fund-raising is all about trust and some luck. I was calling around in December 2012 to fulfill my goal for the year for PrathamUSA. One person returned my call and asked me what I wanted. I told him I was looking for $15,000 to fulfill my goal for the year. He asked me to come to his office and pick up the check. When I went to his office on December 30, he handed me the check and asked me what else he could do for our organization. I told him that my goal was higher for 2013 and I wanted $25,000 from him. He said he would consider it and told me that he owned several hotels in Chicagoland, and if we wanted his hotels for a fund-raising event or our regular meetings, we could use it at no cost. We held our 2013 fund-raising gala at his hotel, and he also met his commitment. We had developed a trust relationship, and I felt confident asking him for $50,000 for 2014. Since then, he joined our board and has continued giving at $50,000 per year.

We raised $20,000 per year with a Children's Read-a-thon conducted by one of our volunteers. The children set goals for the year, and during the summer, they read a lot of books and sent their webpages to potential donors. One eight-year-old was so persistent that he collected $4,200. When I asked him how he did it, he said, "I read a lot of books and kept bugging my donors to help me reach my goal." We also set up incentives for the children by matching their donation when they reached the $1,000 and $2,000 levels.

Trust will be built over time, but the biggest factors of trust are an organization's

- commitment to its mission;
- transparency in its finances;
- ethical conduct; and
- knowledge of inner workings of the organization.

1. Diversification

Diversification of funding sources is very important for a nonprofit to thrive. No organization can stay afloat if its funds are only coming from one source—if (or rather when) that source runs dry, the organization is left without the means to accomplish its mission effectively. The majority of nonprofits' income comes from individual donors like you and me, so it's in the organization's best interest to cultivate your relationship as a donor over time. Time, energy, and funds will be spent to cultivate their constituency base and will be returned exponentially in the form of advocates, donors, and volunteers to their organization.

According to *Achieving Excellence in Fundraising*, linkage, ability, and interest are the three main factors in identifying prospective donors to their organization.

- Linkage—this refers to the connection that the prospective donor has with the agency. This could be an emotional link, a geographical link, or a professional link to that person. Everyone has these bonds with their friends, family, and colleagues; it is more commonly referred to as a *network*.
- Ability—this refers to the financial capacity of the prospective donor to give a gift that is appropriate to his or her income. Evaluation of a prospective donor's ability can be evaluated by the agency (probably through a donor prospect database, if the organization is in a position to pay for it) or by that person's peers who are already connected with the cause.
- Interest—this one seems pretty obvious, but even the wealthiest of prospective donors will not give to an organization if they have no interest in it or feel there is nothing in it for them (whether it be recognition, social standing, or just the classic "warm fuzzy feeling").

People are influenced by many things in their life, and it's the primary job of the fund raiser to determine what those things are and how they fit into the organizational mission. These things include a person's

- family background;
- religion;
- health status;
- hobbies and interests;
- social groups and networks;
- civic and political affiliations/groups;
- educational background; and
- profession.

All of these factors influence a person's values, priorities, and ultimately their ability/propensity to give. These factors shift, evolve, and change throughout a person's lifetime, which may sometimes fit with the needs of an organization, and sometimes it might not. This affects whether or not you're able to give at certain levels (or at all).

If an organization has enough money to invest in a donor database to seek out potential donors, this is the most thorough way that a nonprofit can use to find prospective donors. These systems find a shocking amount of information on citizens, such as annual income, political contributions, educational background, marital history, connections to other donors through former employers or board commitments, and much more. While this may be unnerving to some folks, please know that it is the moral and legal obligation of the nonprofit not to abuse this information. They may not share it with anyone outside of their organization, and usually only senior management is privy to the information internally. They may not use anything they learn for personal gain; they cannot share any of your financial information, nor can they sell the information to any third party without fear of legal repercussions.

Meeting with Fund Raisers

If you decide to meet with a fund raiser from an organization of interest, there are a few things you can expect:

1. Meetings generally happen in a public space (such as a restaurant or coffee shop), and the agency will most likely contribute to the cost of your meal or coffee. Pick a location that's fun, casual, and easy to talk in.
2. Fund raisers (good ones, anyway) will be able to set themselves aside and let the "case for support" do the talking. Asking for money is a nerve-wracking experience for anyone, whether they do it professionally or not. But if the fund raiser is passionate about the mission and understands the needs of an organization, he or she will be able to set nerves aside and let the mission speak for itself.
3. Successful fund-raising means asking for "the right gift" from "the right person" in "the right way" at "the right time." It's a lot more complicated than most donors understand and requires a level of competency of human behavior to gather a sizable donation. Asking for too much money or not enough money can result in a no, as can asking during the wrong moment or in the wrong way—it's a lot to manage!

A fund raiser must be able to articulate several pieces of vital information to you about their organization. This includes (but is not limited to): mission statement, goals, objectives, programs and services, finances, governance, staffing, service delivery, planning and evaluation processes, and history (*Achieving Excellence in Fundraising,* 2011). Let's break these down:

- Mission Statement—this is a statement that describes an organization's predominant values, the circumstances preventing the fulfillment of these values, steps needed to overcome these circumstances, and an assertion that their organization will overcome these obstacles.
- Goals—this describes what the organization's plan is to resolve the problems set forth in its mission statement. There will most likely be several of these goals, depending on how vast and plural their programming is.
- Objectives—one may think that *objectives* and *goals* are the same things, but they are not. Objectives are more specific than goals; they explain *how* the organization plans to achieve their goals. An acronym to remember is SMART:
    - Specific
    - Measurable
    - Achievable
    - Results-oriented
    - Time-determined
- Programs and Services—this is a description of how the organization serves its target populations. This displays that there are real lives that are being impacted by the work of this nonprofit. Fund raisers will usually bring in inspirational stories of clients to demonstrate the effectiveness of their programs and services.
- Finances—this does not mean a fund raiser will provide you with a donation-by-donation breakdown of their organization (nor do you need it). But the fund raiser should be able to demonstrate a general overview of the expenses of the organization that justify the

raising of funds as well as a general breakdown of income sources (usually by percentage of overall budget coming from individuals, foundations, corporations, government, and so on.).
- Governance—basic questions about a nonprofit's governing board should be answered, such as its size, demographics, contributions to the organization, conflict of interest, and participation in fund-raising.
- Staffing—an organization's staff drives all aspects of a nonprofit organization. Skilled, energetic, and dedicated staff members mark a great case for support, and the fund raiser should be able to answer basic questions about the structure and longevity of the staff.
- Facilities and Service Delivery—this should answer the question "How do people access your programs and services?" They should ensure that all people they intend to serve have access to their programs.
- Planning and Evaluation—how does the organization evaluate how successful it is? This area makes it clear whether or not the nonprofit holds itself accountable for achieving its mission.
- History—a nonprofit needs to be able to describe the history of the organization—the hurdles it had to jump over to succeed and how many people it has been able to serve in its lifetime…to "tell the story" of the organization.

There is one item that is essential to the decision to make a donation—you must be able to trust the organization with your money. Be absolutely sure it's the right fit for you and that the agency has a good history of using money responsibly. To accomplish this, you must ask questions! While a fund raiser should be able to explain and comment on all the components of his or her organization, he or she may not be as forthcoming unless you break the ice and begin asking questions. Consider what an auditor or foundation would ask the organization before trusting it with a large sum of money. Perhaps look online at large endowments and see what information they ask the nonprofit to report on after receiving a grant. These will help give you ideas as to what information is pertinent to ask.

Some examples of questions to ask fund raisers include:

- What is your mission statement and what work does your organization do to achieve it?
- What do you plan to accomplish with this money and how do you intend to do it?
- What makes your organization unique when compared to others with similar missions and purposes?
- How does your organization impact the community at large?
- How does your organization hold itself accountable for the work it does and for accomplishing its stated goals?

The Donor Pyramid

The ultimate goal of fund-raising is to move individuals up what's called "the donor pyramid." This moves people up the ladder of donors, and the method of solicitation/method of giving will likely change as you move up.

- One-Time Donor
  First, you may just be a one-time donor. Perhaps a friend asked you to contribute to his or her fund-raising campaign through peer-to-peer fund-raising, and you made a donation once (but have no interest in continuing to support their mission). Most likely this gift was made through an impersonal medium, such as telemarketing, a fund-raising letter, Internet or media source, or a benefit event.

- Habitual/Renewed
  Eventually, the organization hopes that you will become a habitual donor. This might mean you give monthly, quarterly, or annually on whatever schedule works for you. This engages you further with the organizational mission and gives the organization a reliable source of individual income. This likely came from a personal contact, a fund-raising letter (personalized this time), or a phone call.
- Major Donor
  Then, a fund raiser may want to move you up to major donor status. This usually has different meanings for different organizations. Some consider a gift of $500 or more as a major donor, and some consider it at the $5,000 mark. Essentially, this means that it's a sizable enough gift that impacts their work in a major way. Once again, this is probably through a personal contact, personalized letter, or a phone call.
- Legacy/Planned or Capital Donors
  These are the top tier of donors that give the most sizable regular donations. These are solicited through personal contact *only* from upper management. This includes large gifts or gifts in one's will, wherein the donor leaves part of his or her estate to the organization. Fund raisers will work with you very extensively to figure out what level suits your lifestyle, and you will get the most perks as a donor at this level, such as VIP invites to events or public recognition of your generosity.

Once you've agreed to make a gift (and it is confirmed in writing), a pledge is made in the nonprofit's donor management system. These systems may be basic or advanced, depending on the nonprofit's overall budget and staff capacity, but these help the organization to keep track of giving patterns/overall trends, track lapsed donors and keep track of their ever-changing donor base. Once confirmed, the fund raiser will work with you to pay it through whatever method you prefer—credit card, cash, check, invoicing, money orders, and so on.

Tax law stipulates that if this pledge is not fulfilled by the end of the fiscal year, they *must* have written documentation of this pledge for the IRS in order to count it in the organization's overall income totals. However, if you can no longer fulfill your pledge, *do not run!* Let them know that your circumstances have changed, and they will understand. Being upfront and honest about your financial situation will save both parties a lot of time and hassle and will preserve the relationship.

Stewardship

After a gift is made, it is the responsibility of the organization to thank you in a professional and inspiring manner. This may be done in traditional ways such as through letters, phone calls, e-mails, and so on. However, creative stewardship of donors ensures that donors will stay with an organization much longer and that the donor will spread the word about your good work—the more creative the better!

There are several creative methods of good stewardship:

- Handwritten thank you notes
- Thank you phone calls
- Donor appreciation events
- A survey asking you about your donation experience
- Profiles of donors and impact of their work (in regular newsletters)
- Recognition on social media
- Timely recognition and fixes to donor complaints
- Recognition in annual reports
- Donor "welcome" materials for first time donors

Good stewardship may also unlock new features and opportunities to get involved in the organization, such as attending fund-raising events, joining their board, or participating in a committee.

Events

A great way for nonprofit organizations to raise money is through events. Whether it is a large-scale black-tie event or a grassroots dance-a-thon, events are a way for a nonprofit to engage constituents in a new way. Events show appreciation for donor support, raise new funds, and improve the organization's relationship with community partners through sponsorships and in-kind donations. Money from events is raised through ticket sales, auctions, raffles, and sponsorships.

Tickets to events can range from a few dollars to a few hundred dollars, depending on the organization, location, venue, food, activities, entertainment, and special guests. A great way to raise funds for an organization is to encourage your friends and family to buy tickets (or even a table) at an event. This supplies the organization with funds, and you and your loved ones have a great time out on the town!

If you happen to have a relationship with a local business, you have another great opportunity to raise funds for your chosen nonprofit organization. Volunteers, board members, staff members, and donors can all solicit local businesses for donations. This is a good move for these businesses, as sponsorships usually come with the potential for a lot of local exposure, which raises their esteem in the community. Ultimately, this translates into more money for them, because it shows their customers that they care about nonprofits and are civic-minded. Moms and millennials are more likely to buy from a company that displays philanthropic values, so partnering with nonprofits is a very strategic business decision.

Even if a business cannot sponsor the event with money, they can always donate in-kind retail items or gift cards for the event's auction or raffle. This will also increase their exposure as well as get their products into more hands, which results in good word-of-mouth.

Keith Olson shares his experiences with event exposure through in-kind business donations:

> *The local symphony orchestra where I live is always scrambling for funds, and they organize a silent auction at one of their concerts. As board members (all volunteers) we patronize local businesses and encourage the members to seek donations from those businesses. If it's a restaurant or other retail outlet, a gift certificate is perfect, or from a supermarket, a fruit basket. Maybe it's only worth fifty dollars, but the amounts add up, and the businesses get great exposure as the bidders circle the table of offerings.*

Fund-raising for your Cause—Rajaram

Once you have decided on what area or areas where you want to make a difference during your retirement, you can either join a well-established group in your community, become a volunteer for a national or international organization, or fund your dream through grants or crowd funding. There are many national foundations established by corporations and individuals such as the Ford Foundation (www.fordfoundation.org) and Rockefeller Foundation (www.rockefellerfoundation.org). Community funding organizations like the DuPage Foundation (www.dupagefoundation.org) in Downers Grove, Illinois, and Chicago Community Trust (www.chicagocommunitytrust.org) offer funds to organizations working on community needs. You can start a nonprofit organization (NPO) to receive tax-deductible donations from individuals and foundations. This requires filing a 501(c)(3) application to the Internal Revenue Service and waiting for their approval before you can receive donations. Alternatively, you can raise funds for an established NPO that matches your interest.

My friend Dr. Manu Vora almost went blind due to an accident in his school years, and he wanted to do something for the blind people in India who struggle through life. He set up the Blind Foundation for India (www.blindfoundation.org) in 1989 and has since raised several millions of dollars for screening, treating, and preventing blindness among India's poor. This needs a long-term vision and a lot of hard work to make it succeed. So, depending on the passion you carry in your heart, you can achieve anything you want—there are people who will help, but you have to decide what you want and persist in your dream. The happiness you get justifies all the hard work, since you are able to improve lives and give back for all the good things that have happened to you.

The grant-making process is quite similar for all foundations, and an example is provided below from the DuPage Foundation in Downers Grove, Illinois.

1. The grant applications are submitted from DuPage nonprofit organizations to the foundation. This is the hard part where you have to be careful to understand the guidelines and requirements of the foundation and prepare an effective application that states your goals, methodology of achieving your goals, time frame, budget, and how the grant will benefit the community and people.
2. Staff reviews program for completeness.
3. Grant committee members analyze and review applications using the established evaluation criteria.

4. The committee selects the programs that best address needs in the community, improve the quality of life for people in DuPage county, and have the greatest impact.
5. The selected programs are presented to the foundation donor-advised fund representatives to determine the number of applications that can be funded in the year.
6. Foundation board of trustees approves the grants to be awarded.
7. Grant applicants are notified about their applications.
8. Grants are distributed at a fun event.

This shows that it is a long and arduous process to get funded for the dream project that you have in mind to improve the world. However, if you have a dream and can gather friends to share your dream, it is possible to raise the funds you need to achieve your dream.

The basic tenet of fund-raising is that you believe in a cause and will ask others to give to the cause you believe in. The degree of success will depend on your passion and persistence. Many people tell me, "I don't like to ask strangers for money, and I will do only what I can with what I have." With this approach, you can do very little. I did not know I had the talents or desire to raise money for my favorite cause, but when my friend asked me to help with PrathamUSA, I decided to give it a try.

I organized a fund-raising gala in 2010 to showcase the accomplishments of Pratham and raise money from the Chicago community. I reached out to a banquet hall owner of Indian origin, since I knew he helped charities working in India. He agreed to donate the use of his hall and arrange the gala at no cost. I called a dance school and asked the owner if her students could give a performance during the gala. They agreed to do it at no cost. I called many of my friends and requested them to buy the $200 ticket for the gala. With a lot of support from the organization headquarters in Houston, I organized a pledge drive during the gala. A celebrity from India came to help me raise money from the community. With all this help from many people, and a successful pledge drive, I was able to raise $92,000 with minimal expense. I enjoyed the experience, and the funds raised helped almost four thousand children get a quality education in India.

In 2011, I found a few friends who wanted to serve on the local board for Pratham Chicago, and invited the chapter presidents from thirteen other chapters of PrathamUSA to come to a national meeting in Chicago. At this meeting, I met a lot of passionate people who are giving their time, treasure, and talent to the organization so that children in India can get quality education and improve their lives. This spurred me further to look for corporate partners and high net worth donors who could give large amounts to the cause. In addition, I asked one of my team members to look into starting a read-a-thon to motivate the children in Chicago schools to collect money to help their poor counterparts in India. It became a great program nationwide, with all the chapters raising $100,000 per year. I revived the Young Professionals Group in Chicago, and they got involved in mobilizing young professionals in Chicago through fun evening events. In five years, I helped raise funds to educate almost forty thousand children. Of this amount, corporate donations amounted to 35 percent, high net worth donors contributed 40 percent, and the remaining amount was given by small donors. This demonstrates that if you are passionate about a cause and work hard, the community will help you reach your goals. Americans are generous, and this proved to me that you can raise funds for your favorite cause if you have passion to realize your dream.

Fund-raising is an art and requires a lot of planning and hard work. Connecting with supporters and constantly keeping them aware of your cause is critically important to be successful in fund-raising. Maintaining your donor base and managing the donor relationship is important if you want to improve your fund-raising efforts year after year. There are many ways to raise money, but in my experience, the following are important sources of donations that you should pay attention to:

- corporate foundations
- high net worth donors
- government grants
- corporate matching donations for all donors, as applicable

Some organizations will offer to help you collect donations and take a percentage of the money raised. Personally, I am against this kind of fund-raising, since the cost of fund-raising goes up and affects your rating on Charity Navigator. To get the highest four-star rating from this rating organization, your fund-raising and overhead costs should be kept to less than 10 percent of funds raised. Donors are attracted to causes they believe in and also to organizations that keep their costs under 10 percent.

Engineers Without Borders (www.ewb-usa.org) chapters around the United States and Engineers Without Borders International (www.ewb-international.org) serve needy communities around the world. There are many student and professional chapters focused on providing water, sanitation, health, education, and energy to poor communities, working closely with local stakeholders. The chapters use creative ways to raise funds for their projects:

- small fund-raising events in the community using silent auctions, dinners, and the like
- corporate fund-raising among large, medium, and small companies in their country

- corporate gifts of materials and supplies required for development projects
- in-kind and sweat equity provided by the local communities benefiting from the project

In addition to helping poor communities, students from the student chapters learn practical engineering skills and many management skills. Senior and retired engineers donate their time, talents, and treasure to travel to the project site and help the students build schools, bridges, water and sanitation facilities, and solar energy projects for the communities in need. I devote my time and talent every month providing technical reviews and comments on the engineering plans and drawings completed by students. Such ways of sharing their vast experience are very rewarding and give meaning to retired people lives.

Keith Olson's Story

Wherever you want to get involved, there's something for you. Here's a global and local story. A couple in the suburb where I live had a daughter in the Peace Corps in Uganda in about 1995. The daughter went back later to do research for an advanced degree, and her father, Charlie, visited her in 2005. After getting more familiar with Uganda, he got the idea to sponsor students there, as after the early grades, many families can't afford the cost of continued schooling. Additionally, the area, around Gulu in northern Uganda, had been disrupted by the brutality of a group called the Lord's Resistance Army and was afflicted by AIDS. To get money, Charlie and his family enlisted the support of Rotary and had several fund raisers of their own. Check out their organization at childrenup.org. Start-up took more than a snap of the finger—getting 501(c)(3) status takes time, and working in two continents requires patience. Initially there was some local skepticism—groups with fine-sounding names can be covers to take advantage of people. While at least one person of the organization goes to Uganda annually to see how the students are doing, they pay for their travel; 100 percent of the money they raise goes to the cause, and the organization is small enough to adjust to individual needs. One boy had walked thirty miles to get to an eligible school and was given motorcycle taxi fare home. Another, Nancy, is now in graduate school and supports the education of four relatives. Children Up has assisted in the education of nearly two dozen children since 2010, but the benefit is two directional—any of the Americans in Children Up have been welcomed, have witnessed a different culture, and have seen how much good education can do. But there are also difficulties beyond the logistics of selecting the students and matching the grants to their needs. In early 2016, both Charlie and his wife unexpectedly got malaria, doubly unexpected in the dry season.

Will there be a Children Up in your future? That is, will you start a project in another country? Perhaps not, but even if this is too ambitious a goal for you, you can have an impact internationally! Rotary sponsors international projects. Another group I'm familiar with is Habitat for Humanity, as I have been on some builds in the United States and two trips in Africa. Habitat organizes projects in many countries with a focus on supplying affordable housing. If you join a trip, the organizing is done for you, and Habitat avoids areas that are unsafe. You can even organize a trip yourself, with the guidance of Habitat of course. As you are working with local people, you have an experience no tourist would get, though you can add some of the tourist things if you like. In Ethiopia, we took time off from the build to play tourist and visit Lalibela, with its spectacular churches carved into the local bedrock, a world heritage site. In the town where the build work was done, we were treated to a meal served by the community with welcoming hospitality, something tourists wouldn't experience. As a member of a Habitat group, you are a traveler, not a tourist.

On another build, also in Africa, while waiting for materials, I pumped water the old fashioned way, me on the pump handle, someone else managing the pails and jugs. The site had a well—they termed it a bore-hole—but bringing the water was laborious. There was no motorized pump...and labor I did. When the Habitat group was set to leave, one of the women of the community went out of her way to thank me for that effort. I was touched.

If you get to Africa, you'll quickly learn that it's a very diverse place...and very large. If going abroad is a leap too far, Habitat does a great deal of work in the United States and Canada. Whether working in those countries or farther away, their website, www.habitat.org, will point you in the right direction.

CHAPTER 8

Inspirational Stories

The golden years for me (Rajaram) started when I was fifty-eight and decided I had had enough involvement with the corporate world and money making. I wanted to give back actively to communities in Chicago and India. I decided to join the Lions Club in Oak Brook, Illinois, and become more active in helping non-governmental organizations (NGOs) in India. By working with existing organizations that are doing a great job helping the people in need, both in Chicago and around the world, I did not have to start my own nonprofit to achieve goals that were important to him. I am involved with five organizations, three in the United States and two in India, and this has made my life full of purpose; I look forward to every day with excitement. The number of people I can impact with these organizations is incredible. Here is my story, so that it can inspire you to get involved with an organization of your choice.

Lions Club International, Oak Brook, Illinois
I was urged in 2006 by Ashok Mehta, president of Lions Clubs International Foundation (www.lcif.org), to join the Lions Club in Oak Brook. He also encouraged me to partner with Lions Clubs in India to do joint projects in water and sanitation and other development areas. In

the first year as a club member, I boldly suggested to my club that they do a project with the Lions Club in Dharamshala (where the Dalai Lama lives now) for sanitation in a rural part of Himachal Pradesh (literally meaning "the abode of snow"). They agreed, and I started collecting funds from people in Chicago who wanted to help. With $4,000 in hand, I convinced my club to donate $500 and got Lions Club Dharamshala to contribute $500. With $5,000 in hand, the club applied for a LCIF matching grant. Getting the grant was a feeling of accomplishment, with people from the United States and India working together to help people from twenty-two villages in India have clean water and sanitation for the first time in their lives.

The implementing organization, Chinmaya Organization for Rural Development (CORD), worked with the Guru Dhara Self Help Group (SHG) on the following tasks:

- training the SHG to teach their members the proper use and maintenance of the toilets
- explaining the benefits of using the toilets to prevent contamination of surface water and improve their drinking water quality
- helping the people who could not afford to buy materials with the required materials and teaching them to build their toilets
- teaching people who had bought the materials to build the toilets and properly use and maintain them

Thus, a passion to help people was translated into action by CORD, who had approached me for help in the building of 176 toilets in twenty-two villages. Funds amounting to $10,000 contributed by several people (with donations ranging from $10 to $200) allowed him to help CORD provide clean water and sanitation to people in need during 2007–08.

I had another opportunity in 2009–2010 to support a Girls Hostel in Gajapathinagaram in association with the Lions Club of Gajapathinagaram. The woman running the program was Mrs. Sai Padma, a person in a wheelchair all her life since she was affected by childhood polio. When Sai Padma met me in Oak Brook in 2007 and mentioned that she needed help for the poor children in her town, I was impressed with her energy and passion. Working with club and community leaders in Chicago, I collected $3,500 and Lions Club of Gajapathinagaram collected $1,500. Again, with the help of an LCIF match, Lions Club Oak Brook was able to send $10,000 to Lions Club of Gajapathinagaram. Over the next nine months, Sai Padma and her team were able to benefit from a borewell, a water purification system; new toilets; a reading room; a lunch room; electrical equipment; uniforms; and miscellaneous construction items for the hostel.

The hostel educates fifty girls free of cost from sixth to tenth grade. It also serves as an education hub for surrounding hamlets, and the teachers in the hostel help the teachers in the hamlets improve their teaching while finding kids who would do well in the hostel environment. The impact of this hostel is felt in over thirty villages. The hub and spoke model developed by Dr. Sameer Prasad of University of Wisconsin–Whitewater and his students is serving as a model to other rural schools in the region. The children in the hostel are thriving, getting A and B grades, and doing well in competitive exams. Seeing the progress being made by the girls in the hostel and surrounding areas, Lions Club of Oak Brook donated an additional $6,000 to expand the program to more poor children. It is heartening to note that some of the children supported by the club have now graduated and entered into college with scholarships.

This shows that working across the globe with philanthropic organizations multiplies the impact and gets many people with different expertise involved in solving social problems. Organizations like Rotary International and Lions Clubs International are catalysts for Positive Change worldwide and supplement the work of governments in changing the lives of the poor.

FXB Suraksha, New Delhi, India

FXB (Francis Xavier Bagnoud) International is a philanthropic Swiss organization, now headquartered in New York City. It was started over twenty-five years ago to help families affected by HIV/AIDS in poor rural communities around the world. The organization brings about economic independence in such communities by assisting the people in the community to help themselves through livelihood opportunities. In addition, it impacts basic necessities such as water and sanitation, education and health care. I got involved in FXB India Suraksha, a non-governmental organization (NGO), through my friend Gourishankar Ghosh, who was heading the India operations. Supporting them through donations and buying the goods made by people in FXB communities was a start, but when I got the request to help in ten villages in rural Jharkhand state, India, I realized the power of networking among nonprofit organizations and in turn working in partnership with the government agencies.

When the current head of FXB India Suraksha, Mamta Borgoyary, contacted me in 2011 with a proposal to help with water and sanitation in ten villages in the tribal villages of Jharkhand, I was wondering how I could help them, being located in Chicago. The budget for the project was over $40,000. While talking to my brother, I found out that his relative was the head of public health engineering in the state of Jharkhand. I called him and requested that government support the program through leveraging existing government schemes in the area of drinking water and sanitation. He said he had the funds and was happy that a nonprofit was willing to take responsibility for the project. I had Mamta meet my relative, Brij Kishore Jha, and the government provided a letter of support to the NGO. However, the

NGO needed another funding group to pay for its employees and trainers to work with the community members.

I had been working with an NGO called Arghyam (www.arghyam.org) with a mission of clean water and sanitation for all Indians since 2005, helping them start a website called www.indiawaterportal.org. This portal brings the water and sanitation events from around India at one location and highlights best practices and case histories. I convinced Arghyam that working with FXB India Suraksha would give them good exposure and they would be helping a lot of poor people in north India. So far, their emphasis had been poor communities close to their headquarters of Bangalore, India. Arghyam met with Mamta and approved a one-year program to test the model proposed by FXB India Suraksha. Looking at the success and the scope of replication, Arghyam has entered into a three-year partnership with FXB India Suraksha to replicate the project in five panchayats and reach out to twenty-five remote tribal villages in three years. This illustrated to me that partnerships between NGOs and the government and between NGOs in different parts of the country can produce huge benefits to poor communities in India. I feel strongly that such an approach of cooperation is sorely needed to complete projects for helping poor communities around the world.

Engineers Without Borders-India

Engineers Without Borders-India (www.ewb-india.org) is a partner with EWB-International, based in Boulder, Colorado. I (Rajaram) met the founder of EWB-India in 2008, when he was visiting Chicago, and told him that I was a member of EWB-Chicago Professional Chapter (EWB-CPC). The founder sought my help in expanding EWB-India from one chapter to several chapters all over India. Working with his successor and friends in India, I helped them grow to over thirty chapters all over India. I serve on their advisory board and helps them with strategy, fund-raising, and project implementation. The pleasure in working with young engineering students from India and helping them raise funds and plan projects to help the poor with water, sanitation, and renewable energy projects is priceless.

A recent project they completed involved installing solar energy for a school in an impoverished part of Chennai, India. I helped them find funds for the project through the dean of international alumni relations at IIT Madras, India. The sense of accomplishment for young engineers finishing a project to help the poor while still in college is very powerful. "It makes me happy to mentor the students and help them reach their goals.

International organizations like EWB-International are one of the best avenues to use your time and talent to help in the planning and implementation of development projects around the world. EWB-USA student and professional chapters are doing amazing work in the developing world, and if you are an engineer with a passion to help others, joining EWB or similar organizations can be very fulfilling. You come to realize how fortunate you are and how, with very limited funds, you can transform lives around the world. I strongly urge readers to join an organization that suits their interests and spend their golden years making a difference in the United States and around the world.

PrathamUSA

PrathamUSA is a nonprofit organization in Houston helping raise money for the education and vocational training of poor children being done by Pratham in India. It was established in 1999 by a few philanthropists who were keen on improving the quality of education in India. I (Rajaram) was approached by a friend in 2010 to take over the leadership of PrathamUSA chapter in Chicago, and I accepted the challenge. Over the next five years, I had help from many members of the Chicago community to build an organization in Chicago and help raise $900,000 from the community. The Pratham Chicago team accomplished this by doing the following:

1. forming a board of directors made up of people who were passionate about helping poor children in India
2. giving the responsibility to a team of two moms to mobilize Chicago school children for a read-a-thon, and raise money for poor children in India
3. forming a young professionals committee to raise awareness of Pratham's work and raise funds from professionals ages twenty-five to forty in Chicago
4. organizing fund-raising galas once a year to thank the donors and celebrate Pratham's success in India

Before I took up the challenge of working with Pratham, I had no fund-raising experience; I learned along the way with the help of dedicated volunteers in Chicago and other domestic chapters.

Sankara Nethralaya Ophthalmic Mission Trust

Sankara Nethralaya Ophthalmic Mission Trust (www.sankaranethralayausa.org) is the fund-raising arm of Sankara Nethralaya (www.sankaranethralaya.org), a world-class eye hospital network that was started in India in 1977. Dr. Badrinath, an ophthalmologist trained in the United States, started this hospital in 1977 as a small hospital serving the needs of people in the city of Chennai. Right from the beginning, he decided it would be a nonprofit organization serving at least 40 percent of the poor in India. His philosophy was based on three Es—empathy, ethics, and excellence.

I met Dr. Badrinath in 2010 when he was visiting Chicago, and I learned that he was a Lions Club member in Chennai. Since I have been active in the

Oak Brook Lions Club since 2006, I offered him any assistance he needed in getting grants from the Lions Clubs International Foundation (LCIF) in Oak Brook. He told me of a grant application he was contemplating for training the doctors in India (especially the Lions Eye Hospitals in India) for prevention, diagnosis, and treatment of diabetic retinopathy. I then helped him complete the process and get $200,000 from LCIF, and the training of doctors all over India is going well.

In 2015, I was asked by the managing director of Sankara Nethralaya (SN) if I could become a trustee of Sankara Nethralaya Ophthalmic Mission Trust (SN OM Trust) and help them raise money for free surgeries in India for the poor. I took up the challenge, and it has been a great experience. One of the first projects was to organize a fund-raising event in New York at the UN General Assembly Hall. The artist is a popular Academy Award winner, A. R. Rahman. Getting his orchestra group of sixty people to New York from south India, taking care of their needs during their stay, and filling the hall with nine hundred people was an exciting challenge. I was involved in many aspects of planning and execution, and I learned a lot. I helped the SN Chicago team do a fund raising function in Chicago, and we raised money for 2000 free eye surgeries in India. The happiness I get from such unselfish actions is priceless, and I feel good getting up every day to see how I can make an impact in another person's life.

Dr. Prakasam Tata

Dr. Prakasam is in his early eighties, but his energy level will surprise anyone meeting him. He retired after a long career of serving the government in the field of wastewater management. He is focused like a laser on how he can improve the town in India that he left when he was nineteen. He has been an active Rotarian since 2003 and is a member of the Rotary Club in Naperville, Illinois. He has initiated several projects in India with the assistance of his club and Rotary International. Also, with his persistence and pro bono efforts, he cleaned up a large drinking water reservoir that was being contaminated with untreated wastes being discharged into it. He devised a simple, cost-effective way of treating the wastewater before it enters the reservoir. Working with the top official in the town, he got the project completed within a few months and mobilized the college students in the town to monitor water quality and maintain the system he helped design and build.

Since 2006, the projects he has completed in partnership with Rotary International are many. I will highlight a few. The first project was to install a water treatment system and a public sanitation facility in a village near his town, where people were suffering with water-borne diseases. A second ambitious project he undertook with the help of many in the organization India Development Coalition of America (www.idc-america.org) was to install solar lights in forty villages in a rural part of central India. He was able to mobilize $100,000 from various sources and installed this project to create jobs and provide solar lamps to many poor households that were not connected to the electric grid. A third project was to train wastewater treatment plant operators in two cities in southern India, taking with him experts from Chicago who had a lot of experience running treatment plants in Chicago. A fourth project was to install dialysis machines in a city where the poor were dying of kidney disease. In all these projects, he mobilized help from his Rotary Club and from like-minded individuals in Chicago and India who wanted to help the poor.

His nonprofit organization, Bharati Teertha, is helping the poor children in his hometown learn music, making school and college children aware of their responsibilities to the environment, and publishing books on Indian culture and history. He is a constant source of inspiration to many young people with whom he interacts on a regular basis.

Dr. Suri Sehgal

Dr. Sehgal is a philanthropist in Des Moines, Iowa, from where he ran a successful international hybrid seed company. He and his wife Edda Sehgal started Sehgal Foundation in India in 1999 to promote improved agriculture and help the rural folks around India's capital of New Delhi. He was a refugee from Pakistan and had migrated to New Delhi as a young boy at the time of the formation of India and Pakistan. Through his hard work, he succeeded in getting a PhD from Harvard and became a successful businessman in the seed business. When he sold his company in 1999, he decided to put millions of dollars in the Sehgal Foundation to help rural India. Along the way, he has helped many other foundations do great work in India and other parts of the world.

To institutionalize his work and serve as a model to others, he built the Institute of Rural Research and Development in Gurgaon, India. The institute has helped many rural folks in north India and is now spreading their work to other parts of India. The main focus of the institute is to accomplish three goals:

1. Build capacity in the farmers by training them in better agricultural practices, water management, healthcare, and governance.
2. Conduct appropriate research and development to find better ways of delivering clean water to the poor, improve crop yields, and improve livelihoods.
3. Advocate for better policies at the central, state, and local government levels so that all of rural India can benefit from better government policies and improved implementation of existing policies.

The foundation has offices in Des Moines, Iowa, and Gurgaon, India, and its accomplishments are too numerous to list here, but they have fundamentally changed rural life in many parts of India. Dr. Sehgal is a constant motivator for Indian Americans who can give back to their country of origin while being productive American citizens.

Porus Dadabhoy

Porus Dadabhoy is a citizen activist who says, "I believe in better and accountable government in the US and India." He volunteers for the Citizens Advocacy Committee (CAC) in Elmhurst, Illinois. Staffed by community lawyers, CAC seeks to build democracy by working with community stakeholders to strengthen the capacity, resources, and institutions for self-governance. Playing a catalytic role, community lawyers assist citizens by imparting hands-on training in how to use and apply civic, legal, and community-organizing tools to a community-identified cause as well as provide technical assistance, legal assistance, civic education, and mentorship to youth and adults. For example, community lawyers answer inquiries about First Amendment rights to freedom of speech, assembly, and petitioning the government.

Community lawyers also protect public access to the airwaves, the ballot, government records, and government meetings, as well as answer questions about the structure and authority of local government, accountability measures applied to local government officials, ethics codes, and more. Some of the many additional skills taught include how to use the media, build coalitions, and seek administrative resolution of government violations of various laws, including, importantly, the Illinois sunshine laws. Community lawyers teach community members how to flex their civic muscles and practice daily democracy, thereby building citizen-supported, "small-d" democratic communities and instilling skills that can be applied universally to other issues an individual may be energized about.

Porus has been involved in and is currently participating in several community, social, and civic activities in his town, county and state:

- candidate for county board
- candidate for county treasurer
- president of Federation of India
- president of India Development Coalition of America
- voter registrar
- poll watcher
- committeeman in DuPage County
- member of Committee for Gifted Children, District 99
- teacher at North South Foundation

His consistent and deepening involvement with CAC has spanned two decades, both during his career and after retirement. He started as someone who sought out CAC's community lawyering services and gave back by volunteering, then he served as an advisory council member, and he currently serves on the organization's board of directors.

As a long-term volunteer, Porus has contributed time, talent, and treasure over twenty years. On a personal level, he has benefited from the CAC's community lawyering assistance and has observed how communities and government entities are more democratic because of their efforts—pursued with determination, dedication and pride, and assistance from volunteers.

Children Up

Charlie Laliberte, is a resident of Elmhurst, Illinois, who believes in educating the poor in Uganda, Africa. Charlie and his wife have a daughter who visited Uganda in 2005. When Charlie visited his daughter in Uganda, he was struck by the nice people he met and the lack of education in the community he visited. Charlie's daughter went back to Uganda to do research for an advanced degree.

Children Up has been serving the people of Uganda since 2007. At least one person from the organization goes to Uganda annually to see how the students are doing. They pay for their own travel. The volunteer board is made up of eleven dedicated individuals, who donate their time, expertise, and resources. The money they raise goes to the cause.

Children Up is small enough to adjust to individual needs. One boy who had walked thirty kilometers to get to an eligible school was given motorcycle taxi fare home. Two of the students received eyeglasses.

Nancy, Children Up's first sponsored student and a graduate student, is now working for an international corporation in Uganda and is "paying it forward," supporting family members as well as another young woman.

Children Up has assisted in the education of nearly two dozen children since its founding, but the benefit goes both ways—many of the US volunteers in Children Up have been welcomed, have witnessed a different culture, and have witnessed how much good education can do. Sponsors receive student grades and letters. Learning happens in both countries. What started ten years ago has grown from four teachers to hundreds of supporters.

CHAPTER 9

Suggested Action Plan

Since you have read about how to get involved in giving back to your community and the world, and about the tools available to you, here is a plan of action for you to get started right now. This plan can be used to turn your ideas and passions into action. I recently heard the cofounder of Bridge Communities say that he saw a need in society twenty-eight years ago and immediately got his friends together and suggested Bridge Communities to help the homeless in his community. He saw an eight-year-old homeless girl in a church that was hosting the homeless over a weekend and told himself that this was not right—he knew it was possible for the fairly wealthy community he lived in to pitch in and help this girl and other homeless families. He translated this thought into action by calling his friend Bob and telling him that they should meet to discuss the problem of homelessness. A few friends got together, collected a few thousand dollars, and rented an apartment to house the homeless. Today, Bridge Communities is a thriving organization serving more than ten communities in DuPage County, Illinois, with fifty-one partner organizations and serves 131 homeless families. Their activities include housing, mentoring and tutoring, and employment assistance so that these families can join the mainstream society within two years. Such a translation of idea into action is exactly what my suggested action plan is about.

Action Plan

As you get close to retirement or reach a stage in your life where you have time, talent, and treasure to give others, you should evaluate

- your health and how much time and energy you can give to help others;
- your finances and how much you can give to causes of your choice;
- whether or not your spouse is willing to help you in your giving or does he or she want to do other things;
- how much time and effort you want to spend with your family, especially grandchildren; and
- your passion and how you can translate it into action.

This book gives you all the guidance you need to complete this evaluation and launch your career of giving. The authors know several people who have launched into this second career with a lot of enthusiasm and are staying healthy and giving back to communities in the United States and the world. The inspirational stories provided in this book can give you the push you need to get involved and convert your passion to projects you can execute.

Choosing the Charitable Organization or Cause

You can join a charitable organization as a member or as a volunteer. As you have seen from the inspirational stories in chapter 8, you can do a lot of good in the world by joining organizations like the Lions Club or Rotary Club. Several organizations are mentioned in chapters 4 and 5, but there are many more that you can find with a Google search or by talking to volunteer agencies in your community. Talk to your friends and find out what volunteer activities they are involved in. If one of the activities they are involved in is of interest to you, you will have company to start your volunteer activity.

As mentioned previously, the website Charity Navigator monitors nonprofits throughout the United States and ranks them by their efficient use of donated funds. A four-star rated charity is spending less than 10 percent of its donations for overhead costs and maintains transparency and accountability to donors. Less efficient charities get ratings from one to three stars. You can do your own due diligence by looking at the 990 form submitted by the nonprofit to the US Internal Revenue Service, see Appendix A. This form gives the directors of the organization and all financial details of the organization, along with the impact they are making in the world. Read these carefully for organizations that are of interest to you, and if you find one that is making a big impact in the area you are interested in and is doing it efficiently with donor funds, call them and set up an appointment with a local chapter. If there is no local chapter, you can call the main office. Ask them a lot of questions to satisfy yourself that you can make an impact and you have the time to help the organization.

If your interests are international, you can do further research on the organizations and causes mentioned in chapter 4. The opportunities for service and travel are exciting, and you can contact the many organizations that are US-based and are doing very meaningful projects in different parts of the world. One advantage of doing international voluntary work is the opportunity to learn about other cultures and see your dollars go a long way toward improving people's lives. For example, PrathamUSA helps improve the quality of education in India for just twenty-five dollars per child per year. Sankara Nethralaya provides cataract surgeries for sixty-five dollars per patient and helps thousands every year.

Working with Nonprofits

If you don't want to do things on your own but are attracted by a nonprofit that is doing the work you love to be involved in, call them and join their effort as a part-time employee (if you need the money) or as a volunteer to make a difference in the world. Chapter 5 describes how nonprofits work; selecting a nonprofit in your area requires some due diligence and talking to a few people running the nonprofit. Appendix A will help you in doing due diligence. All you need is passion to help and you can find the right nonprofit to get involved with. You can give your time, talent, and treasure to improve the lives of the less fortunate being served by the nonprofit.

There are several different ways to serve a nonprofit as a volunteer. Some organizations are known for more hands-on work (especially environmental nonprofits), which may require you to be in fair to good physical shape. This is a great way to stay active, but make sure not to stretch your capacity too far! A lot of nonprofit organizations really need office work that some may deem less than stimulating, such as stuffing envelopes, addressing letters, cleaning, organizing, filing, scanning, and so on. While this may not seem like very engaging work, it is still extremely important! Most nonprofits do not have the capacity to take care of these loose ends and/or cannot afford the staff time for their employees to do these time-consuming tasks. It is just as helpful to stuff envelopes for an organization as it is to be out in the field.

Another way to serve a nonprofit in a volunteer capacity is to serve on its board of directors. Sitting on a board is a great way to network; it raises your esteem in the community as well as helps the nonprofit get a diverse and experienced set of opinions to help govern its operations. Many nonprofit boards have specific committees or task forces, such as development, marketing, or quality assurance, that have specific niches that you can serve depending on your work background. Boards are always noncompulsory and are not paid positions, but it is still a mutually beneficial relationship. There may also be a "minimum board gift" requirement to the nonprofit, so be sure to ask about that before committing.

Fund-Raising

This is an area in which every nonprofit wants to accomplish its goals. You can get involved in bake sales or other fund-raising events being planned by the nonprofit. You can initiate a fund-raising event for the nonprofit or start a GoFundMe page for them. You will surprise yourself when you realize the things you are capable of and the opportunity to meet like-minded people and raise money for the needy is thrilling. You will learn how to serve on the board of directors, interact with people of various talents, and achieve success in raising funds to help the needy.

You can raise funds from your friends and relatives. Another source of funds is corporate foundations, and if you have worked for corporations in the past, you can reach out to their corporate foundations and obtain money for the cause you believe in. It is hard work and persistence is required to achieve success in fund-raising. You have to dream big and ask for large donations, from $1,000 to $10,000 or more. You have to drop your fear of rejection—you are doing this for a noble cause you believe in, and until you find the right people and corporations that share your interest in the cause, you should persist.

You can choose from one of the types of fund-raising mentioned in chapter 7 and raise funds for the cause. You can assist with end-of-year giving programs. This has become a must for all charities, since many donors write their donation checks before December 31. However, a personal touch is needed to reach out to lapsed donors and others who have not given to your charity. Personal calls, online campaigns, and many other ways are available to reach new and lapsed donors during the November-December time frame.

Starting a 501(c)(3) Organization

The most difficult and sometimes the most rewarding route to help in a cause you believe in is to start your own nonprofit organization. The IRS has guidelines and forms on its website (www.irs.gov), and if you follow the guidelines and submit your application, it usually takes six months to obtain the certification. See Appendix B for more details. If there are questions raised by the IRS about your application, it can take longer. A lawyer may help you with this process at minimal cost or pro bono, and this usually avoids any delay with the IRS. Dr. Praksam Tata (see chapter 8) did it by himself, and it took him a few months to get his nonprofit certified by the IRS.

This is only the first step in the process of collecting funds for your cause. You have to be persistent in reaching out to potential donors and collecting funds. You have to be prompt in acknowledging donations and keep your donors informed regularly as to how their funds are helping people in need. You have to file Form 990 with the IRS annually about funds collected and expenses incurred in running the nonprofit. The secretary of state's office where you live might have its own reporting requirements; you will have to file annually with that office as well.

The ultimate reward is doing the work and helping the many people who are in need. Every life you transform leaves a permanent imprint on you and contributes to your mental and spiritual health. You meet many interesting people along the way, and some of your donors become your friends and could join the board of trustees you establish to run your organization. All these aspects of running your own nonprofit will enrich your life immeasurably. Many nonprofits that started with a few thousand dollars are now thriving organizations helping thousands and millions of people over the years. Examples are the Rockefeller, MacArthur, and Ford Foundations, whose impacts are felt worldwide.

Parting Thoughts

It is our hope that you will be spurred into action to help the many needs in our society. The only selfish reason to do the selfless work needed to help people in need is the pleasure it provides you to see smiles on the faces of people you help and the way it gives meaning to your life. If you keep these in mind as you launch your career of giving after your professional career, it will make every day a day to look forward to, and you will welcome the challenges involved in helping the people you are impacting. It will keep you healthy—physically, mentally, and spiritually. There are surprising benefits to volunteer service:

- Volunteering brings your family closer together when you participate together in volunteer service.
- You will meet all kinds of people, from donors to volunteers to the people in need; this will broaden your network and connect you to others with common interests.
- Volunteering increases social and relationship skills.
- You'll learn new skills.
- Volunteering counteracts the effects of stress, anger, and anxiety, making your golden years some of the happiest of your life.
- Your self-confidence will increase—doing good provides a natural sense of accomplishment, and who doesn't love a free ego boost?
- You can gain a renewed sense of purpose through philanthropy and volunteerism. It adds more zest to your life and can take your mind off your worries and troubles.
- Studies have shown that those who volunteer live longer, because volunteers tend to walk more, cope better with everyday tasks, and have better thinking skills. This contributes to a decrease in chronic pain and reduces the risk of heart disease and high blood pressure. Volunteering may be the cheapest health plan you'll ever be on.

BIBLIOGRAPHY

Armstrong, Alexandra, Financial Planning. Better Investing (monthly magazine), National Association of Investors Corporation (NAIC), Madison Heights, Michigan, October 2015 and additional issues.

Bach, David. Automatic Millionaire. New York: Crown Business, 2016

Bernstein, William J. . The Investor's Manifesto. Hoboken, N.J.: Wiley, 2007.

Bishop, Matthew and Michael Green. Philanthrocapitalism: How Giving Can Save the World. New York: Bloomsbury Press, 2008.

Bissuk, Shari and Timothy S. Church and JoAnn E. Manson, "Why Exercise Works Magic." Scientific American, August 2013

Brown, E. "Married Couples; Charitable Giving: Who and Why." In M.A. Taylor and S. Shaw-Hardy (eds.), The Transformative Power of Women's Philanthropy. San Francisco: Wiley Periodicals, 2006.

Carson, E.D. "On Race, Gender, Culture and Research on the Voluntary Sector." Nonprofit Management & Leadership. San Francisco: Jossey-Bass, 1993.

Carson, E.D. "The New Rules for Engaging Donors of Color: Giving in the Twenty-First Century." In E.R. Tempel and D.R. Burlingame (eds.), Understanding the Needs of Donors: The Supply Side of Charitable Giving. New Directions for Philanthropic Fundraising, No. 29. San Francisco: Jossey-Bass, 2000.

Dalai Lama, H.H. Beyond Religion: Ethics for a Whole World. New York: Houghton Mifflin Harcourt, 2012.

FAO, IFAD and WFP. 2015. The State of Food Insecurity in the World 2015. Meeting the 2015 international hunger targets: taking stock of uneven progress. Rome, FAO. 2015

Friedman, Lauren F., Take Charge of Your Heart Health, special report in Consumer Reports, May, 2017

Gardner, David and Tom. The Motley Fool Personal Finance Workbook. New York: Simon and Schuster, 2003.

Giving USA : The Annual Report on Philanthropy". 2015. Indianapolis, IN.:Giving USA Foundation, 2015.

Jacobs, Sheldon,. Investing Without Wall Street: the Five Essentials of Financial Freedom. Hoboken, N.J.: Wiley, 2012

Kristof, Nicholas D and Sheryl WuDunn. A Path Appears, New York: Vantage Books, 2015

Mesch, D., Moore, Z., and Brown, M. "The Effects of Gender and Generation on Donor Motives and Philanthropic Giving." Paper presented at the Association for Research on Nonprofit Organization and Volunteer Action, Cleveland, Ohio, 2009.

Mesch, D., Rooney, P.M., Steinberg, K., & Denton, B. "The Effects of Race, Gender, and Marital Status on Giving and Volunteering in Indiana." Nonprofit and Voluntary Sector Quarterly, 2006, 35, 565-587.

Moss, Michael. Salt, Sugar, Fat: how the food giants hooked us. New York: Random House, 2013

Nestle, Marion. What to Eat. New York: North Point Press, 2006

O'Neill, Michael. Nonprofit Nation. San Francisco: Wiley, 2002.

Parsons, P.H. "Women's Philanthropy: Motivations for Giving." (AAT 3155889) ProQuest Digital Dissertations, 2004.

Payton, Robert and Michael Moody. Understanding Philanthropy. Bloomington, IN: Indiana University Press, 2008

Pfeiffer, Eric. Winning Strategies for Successful Aging, New Haven, CT. Yale University Press, 2013

Picard, Matthieu and Antoine Letz and Richard J. Davidson, "Neuroscience Reveals the Secrets of Meditation's Benefits." Scientific American, November 2014.

Pollan, Michael. Food Rules, an Eater's Manual. New York: Penguin, 2009

Pond, Jonathon D. You Can Do it! The Boomer's Guide to a Great Retirement. New York: Harper Collins, 2007

Pontzer, Herman, "The Exercise Paradox." Scientific American, February 2017.

Roizen, Michael F. and Mehmet C. Oz. You -- the Owner's Manual. New York: Harper Resource, 2005

Rooney, P., Brown, E., and Mesch, D.. "Who Decides in Giving to Education? A Study of Charitable Giving by Married Couples." International Journal of Educational Advancement, 2007, 7(3): 229-242

Singer, Peter. The Most Good You Can Do. New Haven, CT: Yale University Press, 2015

Tempel, Eugene R., Timothy L. Seiler, and Dwight Burlingame. Achieving Excellence in Fundraising. Hoboken, N.J.: Wiley, 2016.

Tyson, Eric and Robert Carlson. Personal Finance after 50 for Dummies. , Hoboken, N.J.: Wiley, 2016

Tyson, Eric and Robert Carlson. Personal Finance for Seniors. Hoboken, N.J.: Wiley, 2010

Websites:

www.cdc.gov Center for Disease Control

www.nih.gov National Institutes of Health

www.mayoclinic.org

www.dashdiet.org

www.nhlbi.nih.gov National Heart, Lung, and Blood Institute

www.betterinvesting.org National Association Investors Corporation

www.aaii.com American Association of Individual Investors

www.ssa.gov Social Security Administration

www.irs.gov Internal Revenue Service

www.7twelveportfolio.com One approach to placing your funds

www.bbb.org Better Business Bureau - has scam information

www.charitynavigator.org Evaluates charities.

www.snopes.com A fact checking site

www.lcif.org Lions Club International Foundation

www.kiwanis.org

www.rotary.org Rotary and Rotary International

www.nps.gov National Park Service

www.goladderup.org Financial Money Management Assistance

www.entrepreneur.com Starting a company or organization

www.servicespace.org Positive projects

www.dailygood.org Positive messages

www.bbbsa.org Big Brothers Big Sisters

www.mowaa.org Meals on Wheels

http://esc-chicago.org Executive Service Corps - Chicago.

www.northsouth.org North South Foundation helps children in the U.S. with academics and provides scholarships for needy children in India.

www.habitat.org Habitat for Humanity (also very active internationally)

ww.usaid.gov U.S. Agency for International Development

www.diasporaalliance.org The International Diaspora Engagement Alliance

www.ewb-usa.org and www.ewb-international.org Engineers Without Borders

https://water.org

www.rescue.org International Refugee Committee

www.cwsglobal.org Church World Service

www.heifer.org Heifer International, animals for local improvement. Also in the U.S.

www.kiva.org Micro Finance

www.microloanfoundation.org

www.childrenup.org. Supports education in Uganda

www.fordfoundation.org

www.rockefellerfoundation.org

www.chicagocommunitytrust.org

www.dupagefoundation.org DuPage County Illinois (near Chicago)

www.idc-america.org India Development Coalition of America

www.prathamusa.org for education

www.yuwa-india.org, Worksfor youth development through sports and education in India.

www.arghyam.org Arghyam works for clean water in India. Their website is: www.indiawaterportal.org

www.blindfoundation.org

www.sankaranethralayausa.org) is the fund-raising arm of Sankara Nethralaya (www.sankaranethralaya.org), which operates eye hospitals and a research institution in India.

Acknowledgements

The authors would like to acknowledge the many people who made this book possible. The book is based on interactions with many people who helped us give to society and gain valuable experience along the way. It is impossible to acknowledge all the people who have helped in the development of the book, but the following people need special attention.

Vasudevan Rajaram

I would like to acknowledge the time and treasure that my wife, Usha Rajaram, has given over forty years that allowed me to pursue the various projects mentioned in this book. Her patience over many evenings and weekends while I was involved in writing the book is gratefully acknowledged. I have learned from many who have been active in giving back to society, and their inspiration keeps me going every day doing the best I can for others who are not as fortunate as me. Finally, my parents, grandparents, and elder brother Brig. V. G. Krishnan, who were role models for me and encouraged me to always think of the needy and give back whatever I could.

Keith Olson

I would like to thank my parents, who allowed, even encouraged, my assistance in their golden years. They were role models for volunteering with donations of time and money. I would also like to thank the Elmhurst Park District for preserving a patch of prairie in the suburbs on which many a volunteer, including me, spent many hours. And of course, I would like to thank my wife and family, for their commitment to volunteering as well as patience listening to my jokes of many flavors.

Andrea Groner

First and foremost, I'd like to thank my wonderful parents, Brian and Teresa, for teaching me to channel my passion into compassion. I'd like to thank AmeriCorps for the opportunity to volunteer all over the country and build the skills I needed to succeed in the nonprofit field. My friends, teammates, and superiors during my AmeriCorps terms all taught me to be resilient through extreme adversity. I'd like to thank everyone involved with the IU Lilly Family School of Philanthropy for helping to turn me into a better thinker, stronger leader, and more empathetic change maker.

Appendix A: How to Analyze a Nonprofit Entity

Once you have decided that you want to help a nonprofit organization that fits your charitable or service needs, you have to analyze the organization thoroughly to ensure they are doing what they claim in their brochures and other publicity. If an organization claims it has a rating from Charity Navigator, you can go to their website and find out a lot of details about their rating (four-star is the highest for organizations that keep their expenses under 10 percent; 90 percent of the funds received goes toward charitable activities) and how much they collected funds and how they spent it for the causes they are supporting. If an organization is small and you cannot find much information about them from websites other than their own, you can analyze their performance, management, and financial stability by accessing the IRS Filing Form 990, which every nonprofit has to file every year.

The 990 form (www.irs.gov) tells the complete financial story of the organization and how it is managed. Just like a 1040 tells a lot about a corporation or wealthy individual, the 990 lists the following:

1. how the charity collected the money—from individuals, corporate foundations, or government sources

2. how it spent the money—fund-raising expenses, salaries and benefits paid to employees and officers and directors, and so on.
3. details about the charity's governance and management
4. program accomplishments—people served, results achieved, impacts on beneficiaries, and so on
5. assets and liabilities
6. balance sheet, which shows the charity's survivability into the future and how it is spending the money

After you have done the analysis and decided you want to work with a particular charity to support the cause, you can visit them and meet the management team and staff. You can find out about volunteering opportunities, money that you can donate to a particular project that you like, and sharing your talent to improve their operations. If you want to serve on their board, you can find out what the requirements are and if they have any openings coming up.

There are many causes mentioned in the book but there are many more that we have not mentioned. So do your research with all the tools available online and in print. It is ultimately the people who run the organization who will swing your decision as to which organization you want to be involved with and donate your time, talent, and treasure to. Good luck in finding a purposeful cause to support!

Appendix B—Formation of a 501(c)(3) Organization

The IRS allows US citizens to form tax-exempt nonprofit organizations to provide charitable services to the needy in our communities. If you are passionate about starting such an organization to raise funds and implement your charitable work, there are many challenges that you should be aware of before you spend a lot of time doing this and get frustrated. This appendix will guide you through the essential things you will need to start a tax-exempt organization and the ongoing record keeping and filing work that is required by law. Form 4220 (www.irs.gov) gives you detailed instructions on how to file for 501(c)(3) status with the IRS.

The types of tax-exempt organizations are broadly divided into public charities and private foundations. Private foundations are set up by wealthy people (like the Gates and MacArthur Foundations), and some of their wealthy friends and a few other donors contribute to the foundation. Most of us who want to get smaller contributions from many donors set up public charities, and these can be set up as charitable activities to support the needy, educational charities, or religious charities.

The first step is to determine which of these you want to focus on and the scope of the charitable work you want to do. You have to register it in the state of your residence and obtain a Federal Identification Number using Form SS-4. There are a lot of responsibilities for record-keeping and tracking all donations. You have to acknowledge the donations received promptly and file annual returns with the secretary of state in your state and with the IRS. Meticulous records of all funds received and expenses incurred should be maintained. The IRS Form 990 and your application (Form 1023) should be available to the public. If you do not file the Form 990 for three years, the IRS will remove your tax-exempt status.

The IRS takes a few months to review your application and provide a determination letter of your tax-exempt status. While your application is pending, you can take donations, but you run the risk of the IRS not approving your tax-exempt status. You still have to file the annual 990 form while your application is being reviewed. Many people use a lawyer to file the 1023 form to expedite approval, but it is not necessary. However, you have to be clear in your purpose and carefully fill out the form with no blanks.

Finally, running a tax-exempt organization is time-consuming, and you will need help from a lot of volunteers for fund-raising and running your organization efficiently. Make sure you have a large circle of friends who will help you in your nonprofit.

About the Authors

Vasudevan Rajaram has written four books on mining, environment and ecology, and waste management. He has been heavily involved with philanthropy for the past thirteen years. He holds a Ph.D. in Engineering and a J.D. in Energy and Environmental Law.

Keith Olson is a retiree who is actively involved in several organizations in Illinois as a volunteer and Board Member.

Andrea Groner has a Masters in Philanthropy and works at Big Brothers Big Sisters in Indianapolis, Indiana.

www.ingramcontent.com/pod-product-compliance
Lightning Source LLC
Chambersburg PA
CBHW071207240526
45470CB00018B/1533